The **Politically Incorrect Guide**™ to

THE VIETNAM WAR

Praise for

The **Politically Incorrect Guide**™ to

THE VIETNAM WAR

"Phil Jennings has something to say, namely that the historical record, as selectively compiled and presented by the political Left, has done a terrible disservice to the hundreds of thousands of men who fought in The Vietnam War. With great passion, an unapologetic love of his country, and—drum roll, please—the truth to support his case, Captain Jennings walks us through this tragic struggle, the war America never lost, but wasn't allowed to win, either."

　　–L. Brent Bozell III, nationally syndicated columnist and president of the
　　Media Research Center

"In the past several decades, no historical subject has been so grievously distorted by the politically correct as the Vietnam War. Whereas most of the war's chroniclers objected to American involvement at the time, Phillip Jennings was in Vietnam fighting the war, and like most veterans he disputes the antiwar narrative that has dominated the publishing world. His account skillfully weaves together a wealth of historical facts that blow apart the myths handed down by professors and journalists."

　　–Mark Moyar, Ph.D., author of *Triumph Forsaken: The Vietnam War, 1954-1965*

"When I first met Jennings at Camp Lejeune in the 1960s, he told me his ambition was to become the world's first successful right-wing folk singer. He failed miserably at that, but yet, over the last 40 years, he has managed to channel his energies toward successfully defeating political correctness wherever he finds it. This book debunks so many of what our generation's warriors know to be 'The Myths of Vietnam' that it needs to be required reading. Lance Corporal Diogenes, you may extinguish your lamp. Our generation has found an honest man."

　　–Major General Larry S. Taylor, USMCR (retired), former Commanding General, 4th Marine Aircraft Wing

The **Politically Incorrect Guide**™ to

THE VIETNAM WAR

Phillip Jennings

Since 1947
REGNERY
PUBLISHING, INC.
An Eagle Publishing Company • Washington, DC

Cataloging-in-Publication data on file with the Library of Congress

ISBN 978-1-59698-567-4

Published in the United States by

Regnery Publishing, Inc.
One Massachusetts Avenue, NW
Washington, DC 20001
www.regnery.com

Manufactured in the United States of America

10 9 8 7 6 5 4 3 2 1

Books are available in quantity for promotional or premium use. Write to Director of Special Sales, Regnery Publishing, Inc., One Massachusetts Avenue NW, Washington, DC 20001, for information on discounts and terms or call (202) 216-0600.

Distributed to the trade by:
Perseus Distribution
387 Park Avenue South
New York, NY 10016

For my wife, Deborah.
Like a good Marine—Always Faithful.

CONTENTS

Contents

Introduction

THE DEFEAT THAT WASN'T

N o war in American history is as shrouded in obfuscation and myth as the Vietnam War—despite the fact that it was televised at the time, and has been written about at such enormous length that my bookshelves creak under the strain of my Vietnam library. "Vietnam" has entered into our national memory as a byword for disaster, usually accompanied by the word "quagmire," and the specter of the war has haunted our foreign policy discussions ever since.

The biggest myth perpetuated about the Vietnam War is that America lost. However misguided America's leaders might have been in some of their political, strategic, and tactical decisions, we still won the war. We forced North Vietnam to submit to the Paris Peace Accords of 1973. Those accords ended the war and pledged the North Vietnamese to peaceful coexistence with the South. I fought in Vietnam, and I never saw us lose a battle. Ask a North Vietnamese veteran of the war, and if he's honest, he'll say the same—the Communists could never defeat us on the battlefield. If you look at the casualty figures, you can see brutal confirmation of that. The United States military lost more than 58,000 men in the Vietnam War. The North Vietnamese military lost more than *1.1 million*.[1] Who would you guess was the victor?

Look at the geopolitical outcome of the war. Communist Vietnam is dependent on Western aid and trying to adopt aspects of a capitalist

Guess what?

‡ America didn't lose the Vietnam War

‡ Communism did not triumph in Southeast Asia

‡ The Vietnamese people are today one of the most pro-American on the planet

economy—indeed, Vietnam is now regarded as one of the most pro-American countries in Asia in that its young people look to emulate Bill Gates rather than Ho Chi Minh.[2] If you look at Vietnam's southern neighbors, you'll see that they're mostly free and no longer in fear of Communist expansion. Though Laos and Cambodia fell, no other nations succumbed to Communist control; and Vietnam's and Laos's postwar poverty and Cambodia's "killing fields"—a Communist-imposed genocide based on class and politics—have so discredited Communism in Asia that even the great remaining Communist power, China, is itself rapidly liberalizing its economy. It is no longer leading any sort of Communist vanguard of worker or peasant revolution. In fact, China's chief Asian allies are two pariah states of particular stench: Burma and North Korea.

It's true, however, that the people of South Vietnam lost the war, and lost it in a way that is painful to contemplate. It is true that they were shamefully abandoned by a United States Congress that had ousted the president, Richard Nixon, who was the architect of our military victory. That Congress, perhaps drunk with irresponsible power after having defenestrated President Nixon, was insistent on washing its hands of South Vietnam, even if it meant disgrace and dishonor for America and a catastrophe we had fought to prevent for our South Vietnamese allies who were handed over to Communist tyranny. If the Vietnamese people have hope for a better future, it is only because they are looking towards America. Behind them, and still over them, is a Communist regime of reeducation camps and a dictatorship that drove hundreds of thousands of South Vietnamese to risk death in fleeing the country on the high seas.

I've written this book in order to set the record straight—and to settle scores with the pernicious mythmakers of the war. I've written it for my fellow Vietnam veterans who have been so badly mistreated by the media and cultural trendsetters of this country. And I've written it for those too young to remember the war, but who have that built-in "B.S." detector that tells them that the story they get from the media, and probably in school, is a crock. I trust them to recognize the truth when they hear it.

Here is the true story of the Vietnam War, as it actually was, by someone who fought there as a Marine pilot and later as a pilot for the CIA's Air America, and who has made a lifetime's study of the war (and even written a satirical novel about its absurdities). No war in American history is in greater need of a politically incorrect—another word for honest—treatment than the Vietnam War, because the people who misreported the war, hammered vile lies about it into our national consciousness, and now tout its supposed "lessons" are the very same people who created "political correctness" in the first place. Shame on them.

Chapter One

WHY WE WERE IN VIETNAM

It was World War II, the "good war," that got the United States involved in what liberals would eventually want to paint as the "bad war" (though liberals were the ones mostly responsible for our fighting it). Before World War II, Vietnam was a colony of France. During the war it was occupied, with the reluctant permission of Vichy France, by the Japanese—the common enemy of the United States and the Communist Viet Minh.

So in 1945 a handful of American Office of Strategic Services (OSS— precursor to the CIA) agents parachuted into Vietnam to recover American prisoners of war and help the Communist Viet Minh fight the Japanese. Americans fighting on the side of the Communists? Well, you have to remember, at the time we were allies with "Uncle Joe" Stalin and the Soviet Union.

American foreign policy was far less worried about Communist expansion in the waning days of the war (before China became Communist and Communist activities heated up in Southeast Asia and Korea) than it was with the French, British, and Dutch looking to reestablish their colonies. In fact, anti-colonialism had been a sort of bugbear for Franklin Roosevelt, who put Joseph Stalin on a somewhat higher moral plane than Winston Churchill. As Roosevelt put it, "Of one thing I am certain, Stalin is not an imperialist"[1]—unlike the devotedly imperialist British prime minister.

Guess what?

- North and South Vietnam had been divided since at least the sixteenth century

- Communist leader Ho Chi Minh had trained as a French pastry chef

- While Ho Chi Minh's "land reform" program resulted in tens of thousands of executions, starvation, and dependence on foreign aid, South Vietnam doubled its rice production in the 1950s

5

No doubt that was small comfort to the people of Poland, Czechoslovakia, Hungary, and elsewhere, who would gladly have traded Soviet "friendship" for British imperialism. (For those who have forgotten, Communism had an even more murderous record than Hitler's Nazis and represented a far more oppressive and tyrannical regime than your average fascist state. Mussolini's Italy was a libertarian paradise compared to Stalin's Rus-

Viet Minh, Viet Cong: A Communist by Any Other Name Is Still a Commie

The **Viet Minh** (Viet Nam Doc Lap Dong Minh Hoi) were the Communist guerrilla force, founded in 1941, formed to rid the country of the French. After the defeat of French colonial rule in 1954, remnants of the Viet Minh became subsumed by the Communist guerrilla force in South Vietnam originally called Cong San Viet Nam, or officially the Liberation Army of South Vietnam (*Mat tran Dan toc Giai phong mien Nam Viet Nam*) which, for obvious reasons, was shortened to **Viet Cong**.

Legend has it that a South Vietnamese sentry was killed while trying to alert the camp to the approach of the "*Mat tran Dan toc Giai phong mien Nam Viet Nam*" confusing them with the Provisional Revolutionary Government of the Republic of South Viet Nam (*Chinh Phu Cach Mang Lam Thoi Cong Hoa Mien Nam Viet Nam*). South Vietnamese President Ngo Dinh Diem finally said, "Let's cut the crap. They're Viet Cong."[2]

Viet Minh—original Communist guerrillas. Viet Cong—shortened version of name of Communist guerrillas.

The capital of North Vietnam, Hanoi, in rare agreement with Saigon, the capital of South Vietam, officially recognized all guerrillas as Communists.

sia.) Still, even after Roosevelt's death, anti-colonialism remained the fall-back position of American foreign policy, equally popular on the isolationist-leaning Right and the "progressive" Left.

After the war and the defeat of the Japanese who had taken over Vietnam, the country was put into the temporary care of Great Britain (in the South) and China (in the North), though it was still occupied by the French, who'd never fully left. China had not yet gone Communist and was led by Chiang Kai-Shek, America's wartime ally against the Japanese. The division of Vietnam between north and south was neither original nor arbitrary. In the late sixteenth century, the country had been divided by two huge walls above the plains of Quang Tri (in the far north of South Vietnam) erected by the Nguyen family, one of many regimes waging bloody feudal battles for control of the countryside. Before that, until the fifteenth century, 90 percent of what became South Vietnam belonged either to the kingdom of Champa (in south-central Vietnam) or Cambodia. In these earlier years, North Vietnam and South Vietnam were combatants, even trying to pit rival European powers against each other—the South seeking assistance from the Portuguese and the North from the Dutch.

Far from being an established nation, it was actually not unusual for Vietnam to be occupied. For most of (what the West calls) the first millennium, Vietnam belonged to China, and for much of its history after, Vietnam was a vassal state of China. In wasn't until the middle of the nineteenth century that the French displaced the Chinese as the leading power in the region. French influence began with Catholic missionaries—though hundreds of Catholic priests and thousands of their supporters were killed in periodic pogroms ordered by the Vietnamese rulers. These became the rationale for the French to finally invade Vietnam in 1858 in what began as a punitive expedition and became a war of successful conquest. Ten years later, King Norodom of Cambodia sought, and received, French protection from the Thais and the Vietnamese. Once established in the region, the French did their best to stop the Vietnamese from killing each other and succeeded in uniting Vietnamese nationalists against them for the duration of their control over the country.

True to his anti-colonial views, Franklin Roosevelt reportedly remarked to Cordell Hull, his secretary of state, "France has had the country—thirty million inhabitants—for nearly one hundred years, and the people are worse off than they were at the beginning. France has milked it for one hundred years. The people of Indochina are entitled to something better than that."[3] While it is inarguable that the Vietnamese had serious grievances against their French colonial masters and were frequently at odds with them, it is equally true that France accelerated Vietnam's economic development, provided it with export markets and infrastructure, and set up Western schools (though far too few of them) and hospitals (ditto) as part of France's self-proclaimed "civilizing mission." As Mark Cunningham and Lawrence Zwier point out in their book *The Aftermath of French Defeat in Vietnam*, "French colonialism in Vietnam was in some ways less harsh than colonialism in other empires. The Vietnamese who learned French and accepted French culture became members of an elite, entitled to good jobs and education. Some even became French citizens." While French rule favored the sizable Vietnamese Catholic minority, Chinese business owners and the Vietnamese landowner class were also admitted to the "elite."[4]

Ho Chi Minh asked the United States for assistance to defeat the French after both world wars and both times he was ignored—at first because he was irrelevant to American foreign policy and later because Ho the nationalist was also Ho the Communist, and the United States' long term interest in Southeast Asia after World War II was limited to preventing the spread of Communism. It was anti-Communism that put the United States reluctantly behind France in its efforts to reestablish itself in Indochina after the war. In the South this happened rapidly with the Viet Minh being driven from Saigon. In the North, things were far more difficult. In 1949, the French signed an agreement with the Vietnamese emperor Bao Dai, making him the titular head of state over one united Vietnam, though the real power remained in French hands, as did an ever-growing war against Vietnamese Communists. The United States felt itself dragged into not only providing France with economic support, but eventually bankrolling up to 80 percent of France's war effort in Vietnam.

American economic support had ballooned because of events outside of French Indochina, the most striking of which was Mainland China's falling to the Communists in 1949 and Communist North Korea's invasion of South Korea in 1950. Both were stunning developments for American foreign policy. America had long been sympathetic to China (in part because of the presence of American missionaries there),

Never Trust a Pastry Chef

Ho Chi Minh (1890–1969, b. Nguyen Sinh Cung) was born in Kim Lien, central Vietnam, the son of a French-employed school teacher, and embraced Communism while living abroad in England (where he trained as a pastry chef under Escoffier) and in France (1915–1923). He later founded the Indochinese Communist Party and spent a good deal of time in Moscow. Ho Chi Minh was an adopted name. It means "He Who Enlightens," or in the vernacular, "He Who Charms the Pants off Useful Idiots."

and it was shocking when the enormous country fell to the hands of Communist revolutionaries. The Communist invasion of South Korea— a part of the world few Americans had ever heard of—only redoubled the sense of an aggressive Communist menace, and was followed by an American-led United Nations "peacekeeping action" (otherwise known as the Korean War) to save South Korea and restore its borders. Communist guerrillas popped up in the Philippines, Maoist rebels appeared in Indonesia, and a Communist insurgency arose in Malaya. The French were now viewed as a buttress—granted a leaky one—against the Communist onslaught in Asia.

That buttress was exploded when the French arranged to fight the Communists in a set piece battle. The French were convinced that in such a battle they could deliver a mortal blow to the Communists. The mortal blow, however, was to the French.

The French chose as their battleground a valley in northwest Vietnam near the village of Dien Bien Phu. The French began infiltrating troops to the Dien Bien Phu valley in November 1953. The deciding battle took place a few months later from March 13 to May 7. The French felt they were baiting a trap by concentrating their troops in the valley. They were well dug in and had an airstrip for resupply. Their goal was to lure the Viet Minh down from the surrounding jungle-covered hills, and then destroy them with superior French firepower.

This was a miscalculation of tragic proportions, because the Viet Minh did *not* come down from the hills—at least not before they unleashed a merciless rain of artillery shells on the French. The Viet Minh had dragged hundreds of artillery pieces through the jungle and installed them behind the hills, out of sight, and out of range of the French, who now found themselves surrounded, outnumbered, and outgunned. The few fighter-bombers the French had could not dislodge the Viet Minh guns.

For the French, the situation at Dien Bien Phu became desperate. French paratroopers were dropped in as replacements, knowing they faced almost certain death. The airstrip, which was supposed to be the French lifeline, was under such constant fire that no plane could land there. Instead, planes swooped low and kicked out boxes of supplies— most of which fell to the enemy. One of the last flights into Dien Bien Phu was made by CIA legend James "Earthquake McGoon" McGovern—a 260-pound pilot who had flown with the Flying Tigers in World War II and was subsequently recruited into the "Civil Air Transport" (CAT, a front for CIA operations). He had flown CAT support missions for Chiang Kai-Shek after World War II, and later was called to service in Indochina. An eccentric and a legitimate hero, his C-119 aircraft was shot out of the sky while attempting to drop an artillery piece to the French. He famously keyed the microphone to announce to his co-pilot, and the listening French, "Well, kid, looks like this is it," before the aircraft hit the ground and exploded in flames. McGovern and co-pilot Wallace Buford were the first two Americans to die in combat in Vietnam. In 2005 the French government awarded McGovern and six other pilots the Legion of Honor, with the rank of Knight for their service in supplying the French army at Dien Bien Phu.

As the French were being defeated, United States President Dwight Eisenhower wrote a long letter on the situation in Indochina to British Prime Minister Winston Churchill. It can be regarded as the first full and clear statement of why America went into Vietnam.

Dear Winston:

I am sure that like me you are following with the deepest interest and anxiety the daily reports of the gallant fight being put up by the French at Dien Bien Phu. Today, the situation there does not seem hopeless.

But regardless of the outcome of this particular battle, I fear that the French cannot alone see the thing through, this despite the very substantial assistance in money and material that we are giving them. It is no solution simply to urge the French to intensify their efforts, and if they do not see it through, and Indochina passes into the hands of the Communists, the ultimate effect on our and your global strategic position with the consequent shift in the power ratio throughout Asia and the Pacific could be disastrous and, I know, unacceptable to you and me. It is difficult to see how Thailand, Burma and Indonesia could be kept out of Communist hands. This we cannot afford. The threat to Malaya, Australia, and New Zealand would be direct. The offshore island chain would be broken. The economic pressures on Japan which would be deprived of non-Communist markets and sources of food and raw materials would be such, over a period of time, that it is difficult to see how Japan could be prevented from reaching an accommodation with the Communist world which would combine the manpower and natural resources of Asia with the industrial potential of Japan. This has led us to the hard conclusion that the situation in Southeast Asia requires us urgently to take serious and far-reaching decisions.

Geneva [the Geneva conference to settle the future of Vietnam] *is less than four weeks away. There the possibility of the Communists driving a wedge between us will, given the state of mind in France, be infinitely greater than at Berlin. I can understand the very natural desire of the French to seek an end to this war which has been bleeding them for eight years. But our painstaking search for a way out of the impasse has reluctantly forced us to the conclusion that there is no negotiated solution of the Indochina problem which in its essence would not be either a face-saving device to cover a French surrender or a face-saving device to cover a Communist retirement. The first alternative is too serious in its broad strategic implications for us and you to be acceptable. Apart from its effects in Southeast Asia itself, where you and the Commonwealth have direct and vital interests, it would have the most serious repercussions in North Africa, in Europe and elsewhere. Here at home it would cause a widespread loss of confidence in the cooperative system. I think it is not too much to say that France as a great power would be fatally affected. Perhaps France will never again be the great power it was, but a sudden vacuum wherever French power is, would be difficult for us to cope with.*

Somehow we must contrive to bring about the second alternative. The preliminary lines of our thinking were sketched out by Foster [Secretary of State John Foster Dulles] *in his speech last Monday night when he said that under the conditions of today the imposition on Southeast Asia of the political system of Communist Russia and its Chinese Communist ally, by whatever means, would be a grave threat to the whole free community, and that in our view this possibility should now be met by united action and not passively accepted. He also talked intimately with* [British ambassador to the United States] *Roger Makins.*

I believe that the best way to put teeth into this concept and to bring greater moral and material resources to the support of the French effort is through the establishment of a new, ad hoc grouping or coalition composed of nations which have a vital concern in the checking of Communist expansion in the area. I have in mind in addition to our two countries, France, the Associated States [Vietnam, Laos, Cambodia], *Australia, New Zealand, Thailand and the Philippines. The United States Government would expect to play its full part in such a coalition. The coalition we have in mind would not be directed against Communist China. But if, contrary to our belief, our efforts to save Indochina and the British Commonwealth position to the south should in any way increase the jeopardy to Hong Kong, we would expect to be with you there. I suppose that the United Nations should somewhere be recognized, but I am not confident that, given the Soviet veto, it could act with needed speed and vigor.*

I would contemplate no role for Formosa or the Republic of Korea in the political construction of this coalition.

The important thing is that the coalition must be strong and it must be willing to join the fight if necessary. I do not envisage the need of any appreciable ground forces on your part or our part. If the members of the alliance are sufficiently resolute it should be able to make clear to the Chinese Communists that the continuation of their material support to the Viet Minh will inevitably lead to the growing power of the forces arrayed against them.

My colleagues and I are deeply aware of the risks which this proposal may involve but in the situation which confronts us there is no course of action or inaction devoid of dangers and I know no man who has firmly grasped more nettles than you. If we grasp this one together I believe that we will enormously increase our chances of bringing the Chinese to believe that their interests lie in the direction of a discreet disengagement. In such a contingency we could approach the Geneva conference with the position of the free world not only unimpaired but strengthened.

Today we face the hard situation of contemplating a disaster brought on by French weakness and the necessity of dealing with it before it develops. This means frank talk with the French. In many ways the situation corresponds to that which you describe so brilliantly in the second chapter of "Their Finest Hour," when history made clear that the French strategy and dispositions before the 1940 breakthrough should have been challenged before the blow fell.

I regret adding to your problems. But in fact it is not I, but our enemies who add to them. I have faith that by another act of fellowship in the face of peril we shall find a spiritual vigor which will prevent our slipping into the quagmire of distrust.

If I may refer again to history, we failed to halt Hirohito, Mussolini and Hitler by not acting in unity and in time. That marked the beginning of many years of stark tragedy and desperate peril. May it not be that our nations have learned something from that lesson?

So profoundly do I believe that the effectiveness of the coalition principle is at stake that I am prepared to send Foster or [Under Secretary of State Walter] Bedell [Smith] to visit you this week, at the earliest date convenient to you. Whoever comes would spend a day in Paris to avoid French pique, the cover would be preparing for Geneva.

Eisenhower

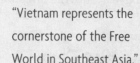

John F. Kennedy and Vietnam

"Vietnam represents the cornerstone of the Free World in Southeast Asia."

Remarks of **Senator John F. Kennedy** at the Conference on Vietnam Luncheon in the Willard Hotel, Washington, D.C., June 1, 1956.
Full text in Appendix A.

The French meanwhile were tired of fighting Communists in Indochina (they did, after all, have plenty of Communists roiling French politics at home). Moreover, the strategic objective of the battle of Bien Dien Phu, now looking grim, had never been to destroy the Communists so that the French could stay in Indochina; it had been merely to defeat, even if only temporarily, the Communist insurgency so that the France could withdraw from Vietnam in some orderly way. In other words, the French were playing for a tie; the Viet Minh were playing to win. France also feared that the armistice ending the Korean War meant that perhaps tens of thousands if not hundreds of thousands of Chinese troops might come pouring into Indochina. Had the United States been willing to make the same military commitment to Indochina as we had to South Korea, the French might have stayed until the battle was truly won. But that was a non-starter. Eisenhower spoke for the clear consensus opinion of the White House, Congress, and the president's military advisors when he said that no United States troops would be sent to fight in Vietnam unless our allies, chiefly the British (who were already fighting their own counterinsurgency campaign against the Communists in Malaya), would agree to enter the campaign with us, and the French would commit themselves to granting absolute independence to Indochina. Eisenhower's position reflected America's own contradictory impulses: we wanted to see the Communists stopped by an allied effort, while simultaneously demanding that our Western allies dismantle their empires in the face of Communist opposition. Or to put it in reverse fashion, as David Bruce, the United States ambassador to France did in 1950, "The ultimate success of U.S. policy depends on the encouragement and support of both local nationalism and the French effort in Indochina. . . . Yet these two forces, brought together only by common danger of Communist imperialism, are inherently antagonistic and gains of one will be to some extent at expense of other."[5] But by 1954, getting the French to agree to leave Indochina was easy; fighting the Communists was not.

In a pattern that would be repeated, the strength of the Communists in Vietnam was not nearly so powerful as the Western powers assumed. The French had, in fact, badly ground down the Viet Minh (despite the self-imposed French disaster-in-progress at Dien Bien Phu), and the Viet Minh were desperate for aid from Communist China. But the Viet Minh were also well aware that opinion in France had turned against the war and that the French were seeking a settlement to leave Indochina. This

Books the Viet Cong Wouldn't Want You to Read

Why We Were in Vietnam, Norman Podhoretz (Simon and Schuster, 1982). The Left continues to protest that they didn't understand why the United States was in Vietnam. They could read this book.

knowledge—and the delivery of heavy artillery pieces, ammunition, and military advisors from Red China—freed the Viet Minh to "go for broke" against the French at Dien Bien Phu. No matter how many men the Viet Minh lost, it would not change their position at the Geneva negotiations. But if they won, France's negotiating position, already weak, would be anemic.

Eisenhower had the United States 7th Fleet offshore and ready, should he decide to intervene and save the French at Dien Bien Phu. But in the end, Britain's unwillingness to commit troops, France's weakness, and his own doubts about fighting another land war in Asia so soon after ending the war in Korea caused Eisenhower to demur. The French were defeated at Dien Bien Phu, surrendering to the Viet Minh on May 7, 1954. The Viet Minh paid a heavy price for their victory, losing almost 23,000 men (half of their entire fighting force) according to Western estimates[6] (more accurate than Viet Minh figures). Eisenhower's decision not to intervene and prevent the destruction of the French army at Dien Bien Phu was a crucial mistake, giving the Communists a victory they should never have had.

In July 1954, France signed a peace agreement with the Viet Minh at the Geneva Conference. Attending the conference were the Kingdom of Cambodia, the Democratic Republic of Vietnam, France, the United States, the United Kingdom, the USSR, the People's Republic of China, the Kingdom of Laos, and the State of Vietnam (French Vietnam, which would become South Vietnam).

The Geneva Accords, which were not signed by the United States, split the country into two parts, divided at the 17th parallel, just above Quang Tri, South Vietnam. Viet Minh units were obliged to return to Communist-dominated North Vietnam, while Vietnamese who had fought for or were otherwise loyal to the French were granted the right to emigrate south. Somewhere between 800,000 and a million people did, many of them Vietnamese Catholics who feared an incipient Communist (and therefore militantly atheist) regime in the north. The agreement also called for a national, free election to be held within two years to determine who would run the unified country.

The Viet Minh were not happy with the agreement but claimed China and the Soviet Union pressured them to compromise and sign. Mark Moyar in his book *Triumph Forsaken* disputes this account, saying that the Viet Minh had confided to the Soviets and Chinese that partition was the best possible outcome as their heavy losses at Dien Bien Phu made it desirable to gain a peace "for rebuilding the army before pursuing other gains."

Watch Out if a Country Adds "People's" or "Democratic" to Its Name

First, you just need to remember **North Vietnam** (Communist; enemy to U.S. except for Left/ liberals) and **South Vietnam** (Non-Communist; supported by people with common sense).

The Republic of Vietnam (originally the "State of Vietnam") was recognized internationally in 1950. Its capital was Saigon until 1975 when the name was changed to Ho Chi Minh City after North Vietnam conquered South Vietnam in what the U.S. liberals refused to call an invasion, lasting roughly twenty years. America supported the Republic of Vietnam.

The Democratic Republic of Vietnam (DRV) was created by Ho Chi Minh after the defeat of the French at Dien Bien Phu in 1954. Its capital is Hanoi. North Vietnam was the first Communist state in South-East Asia. China and Russia supported the DRV.

The later-described "weariness with the war" in the U.S. might have been partially caused by trying to keep up with who in the heck was fighting whom.

The State of Vietnam, ruled at the time by Bao Dai, was vehemently against the agreement because a "free" election would be impossible given that the Communist half of Vietnam was the more highly populated and that the Communists would determine how the people in the North voted. The United States agreed with Bao Dai that the idea of free elections was a pipe dream. The United States, however, did not agree that Bao Dai should rule South Vietnam. America wanted a South Vietnamese leader untainted by French colonialism and supported Bao Dai's prime minister Ngo Dinh Diem, a powerful politician, who, though Catholic, had a strong record as a Vietnamese nationalist.

From the point of view of South Vietnam, the Geneva Accords had been essentially between two parties—France and the Viet Minh—neither of whom had any legal right to agree about the future of Vietnam. A South Vietnamese delegation led by Ngo Dinh Diem had, like the United States, not signed the Accords. Diem thought it wrong to consign half of Vietnam to the Communists. As a Catholic he wanted a Vietnam that was united on the side of the West and not under atheistic Communist tyranny.

Vietnam 1954–1960 (Nation Building 101)

In September 1954, in order to shore up regional security, the United States organized a regional defense alliance, called the Southeast Asia Treaty Organization (SEATO). Its members included France, Australia, New Zealand, Pakistan, the Philippines, Thailand, the United Kingdom, and the United States. The countries of Laos, Cambodia, and Vietnam were prohibited from joining due to provisions in the Geneva agreements; they were listed as "protected nations." Meeting in Manila, the United States gave a pep talk to its allies that Communism should be halted in Southeast Asia. The treaty was enthusiastically ratified by the United States Senate with only one opposing vote. There was little if no disagreement in the U.S. that the Communists must be stopped.

At best, SEATO was a forum for reporting on and discussing Communist aggression in the region. It pledged its members to consult with one another about any common danger. It did not require any member state to come to the military defense of any country or government in the region. (In 1977, SEATO, having outlived any usefulness it ever had, was dissolved.)

The playboy and the priest

Far more important than SEATO was Ngo Dinh Diem. No figure—not Ho Chi Minh, not Lyndon Johnson—was more important to the outcome of events in Vietnam than Diem. He balanced the basic paradoxes of the war: Asian standards vs. Western standards; realism vs. idealism; abstract political maneuvering vs. bloody reality. Americans in Vietnam who were comfortable dealing with foreigners and foreign cultures generally accepted Diem as the best man we had. Americans who believed that our support for Diem required him to act like an American politician (and this included most of the State Department) thought Diem was neither a good nor even a decent choice to be "our man in Vietnam."

He came into office in 1954, when Bao Dai, the former emperor (1926–1945) turned chief of state of non-Communist Vietnam, selected Diem to become his prime minister. Bao Dai had been "drafted" by the French in 1948 to represent Vietnam since they needed someone they could "negotiate" with. The former emperor was a weak, pliant figure, known best as "the playboy of Hong Kong," and his selection was widely seen as a French attempt to maintain control over the country while appearing to be moving toward granting it independence. At the 1954 Geneva Conference, Bao Dai knew he was in over his head and turned to Diem for help.

Diem was an upper class, French-educated nationalist, who had worked in the French civil service in Vietnam in the 1920s and early 1930s. The French admired his strong anti-Communist beliefs and the effective way he handled his duties, and in 1933 made him interior minister to Bao Dai, but they were appalled at his desire for a Vietnamese legislature. After only three months, Diem resigned, believing Bao Dai was a tool of the French. From then on, Diem collaborated neither with the French colonists nor the Japanese occupiers (though he had encouraged the Japanese to lead a Vietnamese nationalist struggle against France in 1942, and in 1945 considered a Japanese offer to become prime minister).

After his restoration, Bao Dai had asked Diem to become Prime Minister on three separate occasions, but Diem always declined, until 1954, when he accepted, with the proviso that he have complete control over the military and all political decisions, leaving Bao Dai as only a symbolic head of state. Bao Dai reluctantly accepted.

Though his appointment was popular, at least initially, with Democratic U.S. senators like Mike Mansfield and John F. Kennedy, who were early supporters, Diem never intended to rule according to the dictates of Western democracy. Diem believed Western-style democracy was inappropriate for a country that had always been dominated by an authoritarian political culture. Nevertheless, there was a stark divide in his own mind—and in reality—between a conservative, authoritarian, Western-leaning government and a Communist tyranny. One was on

A Very, Very Brief Chronology of the Vietnam War

1954 Viet Minh (Communists/nationalists) led by Ho Chi Minh defeat the French

1955 Viet Minh begin terrorist attacks in President Diem's South Vietnam (created in Geneva settlement)

1961 President Kennedy begins building up American presence in South Vietnam with advisors and Special Forces troops

1965 President Johnson sends in the Marines, beginning American troop buildup that eventually reaches 500,000

1969 President Nixon begins drawdown of American troops

1973 All American combat troops are out of Vietnam after ceasefire

1975 North Vietnamese Communists invade and conquer South Vietnam

the side of religion, tradition, and relative economic and civil freedom; the other crushed religion, tradition, and any sort of freedom at all.

Was Diem the logical choice to lead South Vietnam? Ho Chi Minh evidently thought so. He had offered Diem a position in his own regime. Diem refused to even consider it. Not only was he staunchly anti-Communist, one of his brothers had been killed (buried alive) by the Viet Minh. (Diem himself had been held as a prisoner by the Viet Minh after World War II and survived Communist assassination attempts.) Diem was most likely the *only* South Vietnamese with a chance of leading the country in a very difficult time.

In his ubiquitous white suits and carefully groomed hair, Diem seemed at times a "dandy," but he was in reality almost monk-like in his personal habits, sleeping on a cot in the palace, and never marrying. (He had briefly studied for the priesthood and his elder brother became a bishop.) Portrayed in the press as obtuse and tyrannical, Diem was soft-spoken and normally calm and collected. He was, however, extremely distrustful of people—not surprising given what a life in Vietnamese politics entailed—and didn't like to delegate authority. His brother, Ngo Dinh Nhu, was his alter-ego, brash, emotional, vindictive, with a flamboyant wife who was extremely unpopular. Nhu served as gatekeeper, confidant, and protector for Diem. Pressured by all sides, friend and foe, to remove Nhu from a position of power in the government, Diem steadfastly refused for the next eight years. Nhu once told an American journalist: "Every government has to have the tough guy, the man who does the dirty and unpleasant work. Even Eisenhower had to have a Sherman Adams [Eisenhower's chief of staff], in a country as advanced and unified as the United States of America. In Vietnam, where violence and virulence are everywhere, I am the person who takes on the unpleasant jobs. It is I who is vilified, so that others may be spared."[7]

When Diem stepped in as Prime Minister in 1954 he inherited a country in turmoil, to say the least, a veritable "mishmash of conflicting political cliques and religious factions, an ineffective and almost non-existent governmental apparatus, and a farce for a police force and an army," as Phillip Davidson put it.[8] The French, who were still very much present in South Vietnam in 1954, detested Diem, the Viet Minh hated him, the North Vietnamese government despised him, the South Vietnamese religious (and paramilitary) sects—the Cao Dai and Hoa Hao—couldn't stand him, the Binh Xuyen pirates and gangsters (who became Communist allies) fought against him, the Buddhists resented him, and the military wasn't loyal to him. His only solid base of support was among the Catholic Vietnamese. Few leaders in history have acceded to power peacefully with the deck so stacked against them; and yet for all his unpopularity (and he did not think popularity was necessary to lead an Asian country) he was the most experienced, respected, and unifying leader South Vietnam had.

President Eisenhower and his secretary of state, John Foster Dulles (who had met Diem and liked him), decided to support the South Vietnamese prime minister, and in doing so they had broad bipartisan support.[9] Eisenhower ordered the CIA, Department of Defense, and the State Department to work out a program to strengthen South Vietnam's army, and committed the United States to a massive economic aid program to Vietnam. It was an American belief that if the people of South Vietnam enjoyed prosperity, they would be less likely to join the Communists, and, in turn, South Vietnam's relative prosperity would encourage the North Vietnamese to join the capitalist world.

Diem began to build his power base as most Third World leaders did and do—by using bribery, nepotism, favoritism, and sometimes brutality. Although his methods were considerably less harsh than those of the Stalinist Ho Chi Minh—whose Soviet and Communist Chinese backers endorsed any and all means to achieve a Communist state—Diem was held to a higher standard by the French, the Americans, the press, and the Saigon intelligentsia. Diem tried to shore up his position by using American aid to build an army that was loyal to him; unfortunately, his foreign aid largesse built an army that was loyal to bribery, with weak, corrupt leaders, and little fortitude or discipline for fighting.

Diem's initial problems were with the French, who regarded him as a traitor to French Indochina. Diem, for his part, criticized the French for abandoning North Vietnam to the Communists at Geneva. The French wanted pro-French Vietnamese included in Diem's government. Diem not only ignored French advice but purged French supporters from positions of power.

In an interview in 1981, William Colby, who had been in charge of the CIA's operations in Southeast Asia for much of the war, and had been Director of Central Intelligence from September 1973 to January 1976, noted, "The key to Vietnam was that the French had really supported opponents of Diem during the struggle for power in the mid-fifties. And he defeated them. They first supported the chief of the Army, and one of Diem's first moves was to fire him, and that caused quite a tremor at the time. But once he got hold of the army and his own men in charge of the army, then he moved against the police.... When he got those under control, he moved against the various sects, and the French had connections with all of these of course, for years. Their technique of running the colony of Vietnam... was the usual kind of relationship with all the different forces in the game, and not having it unify as a Vietnamese nation because that would get out of their control. So Diem was correct in being suspicious of the French."[10]

Indeed in November 1954, just three months after Diem took office, General Nguyen Van Hinh, commander of the Bao Dai army (one of three major religious/paramilitary sects operating in Saigon), began talking openly about replacing Diem with Prince Buu Hoi. The French supported the idea. But the Americans were dead set against it, and Eisenhower warned General Hinh that American support would end if there was a coup against Diem. The plot disbanded, and Bao Dai exiled Hinh to Paris. Thus began an almost decade-long comedic parade of military officers, government officials, and influential civic leaders into the American embassy, demanding, cajoling, requesting, begging, and suggesting various coups against Diem. Those serious enough to reach Washington got the same reply—aid is shut off if Diem goes.

The Road Not Taken

One of Diem's apparent major military successes was shutting down the Communist supply lines from North to South Vietnam. Unfortunately, this "victory" only diverted the North Vietnamese to build the Ho Chi Minh Trail through "neutral" (really, Communist-neutered) Laos.

General J. Lawton Collins, sent to South Vietnam as a political troubleshooter by President Eisenhower, was initially unimpressed by the prime minister: "Diem is a small, shy, diffident man with almost no personal magnetism. He evidently lacks confidence in himself and appears to have an inherent distaste for decisive action." Historian Mark Moyar points out that these were almost the exact words the French used to describe Ho Chi Minh after World War I. "Like those Frenchmen," Moyar writes, "Collins mistakenly assumed that the Vietnamese prized tall, outgoing, and self-confident men as Westerners did. Within a few months Collins would come around to admire Diem's personality, saying that 'Diem's integrity, strong nationalism, tenacity, and spiritual qualities render him the best available Prime Minister to lead Vietnam in its struggle against Communism,'" an opinion shared by many American advisors who came to know him.[11]

An irony that constantly hung over Diem was his critics' accusation that he was just a puppet of America, while the charge most often leveled at him by the U.S. State Department was that Diem wouldn't follow orders, directions, or recommendations. The decisive factor in shaping

American opinion on Diem was the American press, which would eventually turn with a fury against this "diffident" little man who was, in fact, nobody's puppet.

Diem, it should not be forgotten, was a man fighting a multi-pronged war. There was a savage war against the remnants of the Viet Minh. He was surrounded by a political nest of vipers. There was the Binh Xuyen gangster organization that began with piracy, expanded into Mafiosi-like violent crime, and ended up as recruits for the Viet Cong. There were the paramilitary armies of the eccentric Cao Dai and Hoa Hao religious sects. All these he succeeded in driving out of Saigon with remarkable efficiency in the mid-1950s. In fact, he soon felt so secure—having driven his enemies before him—that he called for a national referendum to determine whether Vietnam would remain a monarchy under Bao Dai or become a republic with Diem as president. The outcome was never in doubt. Diem's own police force supervised the election in October 1955.

Diem the Democrat

Diem might not have believed in utterly free and fair elections, but then again, "Landside" Lyndon Johnson and JFK's Democratic machine weren't exactly paragons either. Vote early and vote often was more like it.

It was an effective campaign. He won with 98.2 percent of the vote. In some electoral districts he received more votes than there were registered voters. Diem wasn't concerned about the appearance of propriety or impropriety. His vote count let the people know that he had suppressed his opponents, which, he believed, would be considered a mark of strength in Vietnamese eyes (rather than corruption, as in American eyes). Diem ousted the French-installed emperor and made himself president.

The next big hurdle was the national elections agreed to by the French and the Viet Minh in the Geneva Accords. The Americans suggested to Diem that he move ahead but insist on strict rules and protections to ensure a free vote. But by their electoral practices, both Ho Chi Minh and Diem had proven that they had no interest in free votes. The process of gaining power had no moral content for them; what mattered was having the power and using it to either extend Communism the length of Vietnam (Ho Chi Minh's goal), or to defend the traditions and relative freedoms of South Vietnam and possibly, in the future, restore them to the North (Diem's goal). On July 16, 1955, Diem said over Saigon radio, "We did not sign the Geneva accord. We are not bound in any way by these agreements, signed against the will of the Vietnamese people." Diem continued, "If proof is not given that they [the North Vietnamese] put the superior interests of the national community above those of Communism; if they do not renounce terrorism and totalitarian methods; if they do not cease violating their obligations as they have done in preventing our countrymen of the North from going south," there would never be any elections uniting North and South Vietnam.[12] The idea of having free elections, or making any accommodations, with Communists (whose method was terrorism, and whose aim was tyranny) was, Diem believed, an absurdity.

J.F.K.'s View of the "National Elections" Proposed by the Geneva Accord

"…and I include in that injunction a plea that the United States never give its approval to the early nationwide elections called for by the Geneva Agreement of 1954. Neither the United States nor Free Vietnam was a party to that agreement—and neither the United States nor Free Vietnam is ever going to be a party to an election obviously stacked and subverted in advance, urged upon us by those who have already broken their own pledges under the Agreement they now seek to enforce."

Remarks of **Senator John F. Kennedy** at the Conference on Vietnam Luncheon in the Hotel Willard, Washington, D.C., June 1, 1956

Diem's views seemed to prove themselves in practice. South Vietnam in the late 1950s enjoyed relative peace and freedom: the Communist remnants of the Viet Minh in the South appeared largely defeated. The American Military Assistance Advisory Group (MAAG), which had taken over from the French in training and equipping the Vietnamese army, felt that steady progress was being made. And Hanoi's primary objective was not in reigniting the Viet Minh and putting them on a war footing, but tightening its own control over North Vietnam. The Communist government advised the Viet Minh to bide their time and content themselves for now with carrying out acts of terrorism and subversion in the countryside. The great war of liberation would come—but not yet.

Before war (what Americans would call The Vietnam War) came, South Vietnam was making tremendous progress. William Colby remembers that "what was really happening was the total social and economic regeneration of South Vietnam. That's what happened between 1956 and 1959. I went to little schools out in the country being dedicated down in the swamps of Ca Mua. . . . I went to the provincial capital, to the office of education there, after having been there and looked at the map. You know, they had a comparative map of the number of schools they had in 1954, which was about two or three, all in the capital or the district capitals, and the number of schools they had in 1959—this was in the spring of 1959—which was on the order of thirty or forty in the province."[15]

On July 7, 1959, the *New York Times* commemorated the five years of Diem's presidency proclaiming, "A five year miracle, not a 'plan,' has been carried out. Vietnam is free and is becoming stronger in defense of its freedom and of ours. There is reason, today, to salute President Ngo Dinh Diem."[16]

Diem was making dramatic economic and social gains for the people of South Vietnam, but he was having far less success building an army to defend his country. Though the Communist insurgency had, temporarily, been laid low, the officer corps of South Vietnam's army remained poorly trained and disciplined, and the ranks were no better; they were certainly no match for the highly disciplined and rapidly expanding army of North Vietnam and its militarized society. American military advisors had to train the South Vietnamese army both in conventional warfare—to meet

Ho, Ho, Ho Chi Minh: How Much Rice Did You Eat Today?

One of Ho's problems was a famine that began in 1955. Flooding and the vagaries of Communist land reform—which inevitably link collective farming, the executions of tens of thousands of uncooperative farmers and peasants, and starvation—had Hanoi appealing to its Communist patrons for assistance. The Soviets shipped the North Vietnamese 173,000 tons of rice and the Chinese added another 32,000 tons.[13]

North Vietnam's land reform program was so obviously disastrous that the Communist Party's Central Committee felt the need to confess its errors publicly. Ho and Giap went from village to village apologizing, trying to pacify farmers who had seen their lives ruined and their friends and relatives killed or starved. Ho tried to appease the intellectuals in Hanoi with a brief easing of restrictions on political and artistic expression. After three months, the Party revoked the liberal reforms and returned to Communist business as usual.

In the South, agriculture rebounded during Diem's regime. In 1954 the production of rice had sunk to 2.6 million tons. By 1959, South Vietnam was producing 5 million tons a year. Rubber production was up, and the number of cattle, water buffalo, and pigs rose from 1.3 million to over 5 million.[14] The quality of life had also improved with the opening of hundreds of new schools and new hospitals, many of the latter staffed with American-trained nurses.

an invasion from the North—and in counter-insurgency against Communist guerrillas. This was a daunting task, as the chief of staff of the South Vietnamese Army observed in 1956, "[I am] certain that many of our units would disappear into the countryside at the very start of the reopening of hostilities."[17]

Hostilities were not far away. As Phillip Davidson writes in his book *Vietnam at War*, "In 1957 and 1958 the Communists admitted that Diem had 'truly and efficiently destroyed our party.'"[18] In 1959, the Central Committee decided to launch an armed insurrection in South Vietnam. In July, some 4,000 trained soldiers began infiltrating into South Vietnam. In 1960, the North "publicly announced its support of the insurgency in the South."[19] The war had begun and we, as advisors at least, were already in it.

Chapter Two

CAMELOT IT WAS NOT

America's new president in 1961 was John F. Kennedy—young, vigorous, charismatic, and pledged to go anywhere and lift any burden to support the cause of freedom. He surrounded himself with brilliant men, rallied our allies, and warned our enemies. And he was challenged almost immediately with the Bay of Pigs crisis—a bungled CIA-sponsored attempt to invade Cuba (Kennedy called off scheduled air strikes to try to feign that the United States was not involved) and overthrow Castro. This fiasco helped convince the Communists that Kennedy talked big but carried a puny stick.

In June, Kennedy went to Vienna for a two-day summit with the leader of the Soviet Union, Nikita Khrushchev, a brash, bellicose man who resembled a cross between Mr. Clean and the Pillsbury Doughboy, and whose persona was the vulgar proletarian opposite of the urbane aristocratic Kennedy. Kennedy hoped to discuss a nuclear test ban treaty and the neutrality of Laos. The meeting did not go well for the president. He was hardly able to get a word in edgewise as Khrushchev shouted him down with denunciations of capitalism and the West, and Michael Moore-like accusations that America was run by a few wealthy businessmen. Communism, Khrushchev declared, was the wave of the future, and its cultural and economic achievements would bury the United States. Amidst all this froth and lather, Khrushchev attacked Kennedy for

Guess what?

‡ President John F. Kennedy's rousing rhetoric in defense of liberty was usually followed up by indecision and waffling in practice

‡ America's commitment to Vietnam was initially a bipartisan effort—though all the troop escalations were made by Democrats

‡ The Kennedy administration encouraged a coup in South Vietnam that removed the only effective politician the country had

even suggesting that the United States had a vested interest in Laos, though he did eventually accept the idea of Laos as a neutral party in the Indochinese conflict—especially as he knew, or assumed, that its neutrality would be observed by one side (the American/South Vietnamese side) and not the side of Ho Chi Minh. The summit was an inauspicious start for the leader of the Free World.

After the summit, Kennedy stopped in London and met with British Prime Minister Harold Macmillan. In a letter to the queen, Macmillan gave his impressions: "The President was completely overwhelmed by the ruthlessness and barbarity of the Russian premier. It reminded me in a way of Lord Halifax or Mr. Neville Chamberlain trying to hold a conversation with Herr Hitler."[1]

Just weeks before Kennedy made his inaugural pledge that "We will pay any price, bear any burden, meet any hardship, support any friend, oppose any foe to assure the survival and success of liberty,"[2] Nikita Khrushchev had announced that the "Soviet Union would support wars of national liberation."[3] Khrushchev's rhetoric was not nearly so poetic or inspiring as Kennedy's, but the fear was that it might have more force behind it.

With the Soviets bullying, blustering, and bluffing (erecting the Berlin Wall, sending nuclear missiles to Cuba and then withdrawing them, igniting and fanning the flames of Third World Communist "liberation" movements, and threatening to defeat the United States in every field of endeavor), Kennedy looked for a place to show his resolve. He chose Southeast Asia.

Sideshow in Laos: Instructive history ignored

In the pre-inaugural briefings between Eisenhower and Kennedy, the Southeast Asia discussion was primarily about Laos, not South Vietnam. The Geneva Accords were supposed to have guaranteed an end to the

Communist insurgency in Laos in return for Laotian independence, but the Pathet Lao (the Laotian Communists) had pressed ahead with their subversion and violence against the Laotian constitutional monarchy. The monarchy was supported by the French, and then later by the United States as we inherited France's post-colonial responsibility for defending the government from the Communists.

North Vietnam was the conduit for military supplies and advisors to the Pathet Lao. Many of these military advisors were Vietnamese, others were Soviets (who also supplied aircraft), but most were Chinese Communists. The Red Chinese had designs on Thailand and saw a possible invasion route over Laos's rugged mountains—and they certainly did not want a non-Communist country, like royalist Laos, on their border.

In Laos itself, the political situation reflected a shifting array of forces that divided into at least three parts: the rightists, backed by Eisenhower and the United States, were led by General Phoumi Nosovan; the neutralist element was led by Souvanna Phouma, who received some American aid, but who sometimes sided with the third faction, the Pathet Lao, who were led by his half-brother, Prince Souphanouvong. In 1960, Captain Kong Le, a paratrooper representing the neutralist faction, led a successful military coup against the rightist government. The United States continued to voice support for the rightists, whom we regarded as the

Pick Your Team

For a detailed view of the relevant political/military history of Laos (1954–1961) one should begin with Bernard Fall's *Anatomy of a Crisis* (Doubleday, 1969). Keep a scorecard handy—the players are brothers, half-brothers, princes, common soldiers, Soviets, Americans, and of course the ubiquitous North Vietnamese Army, fighting in yet another country they had no right to be in. Having them in your country to help get rid of, say, the French, is like inviting the IRS into your company to help fire a secretary. Basically, the rightists favored support from the West, the Pathet Lao sought help from the Soviet Union and Communists, and the neutralists wanted everybody not Laotian to just go home, although their alliance could shift with the times and events.

legitimate government, while the neutralists allied themselves with the Pathet Lao, the Russians, and the Communist Chinese. The neutralist/Pathet Lao alliance, however, could not subdue the entire country, as there remained large pockets of armed resistance, especially among the Hmong, a fiercely anti-Communist mountain tribe. What resulted was a see-sawing Laotian civil war.

Domino Already Played

At the Geneva Convention in 1954, when the Communist Viet Minh were given North Vietnam, Phoui Sananikone, head of the Laotian delegation, made a statement which the anti-war activists in the U.S. never bothered to read (it being too much trouble to actually research what and who caused the war in Southeast Asia, evidently). Speaking of his country, Sananikone said:

> Withdrawal of the foreign invading troops [North Vietnamese] would mean *de facto* the cessation of hostilities there...Laos is independent. On October 22, 1953, it signed with France a treaty of independence and association of which Mr. Molotov [the Russian] and Mr. Dong [head of the Viet Minh delegation] appear to be ignorant....We have said, and we repeat, that the military operations in Laos are the work of Viet-Minh troops, that is to say of troops foreign to the country in race, tradition, and ideology. We maintain that the so-called "free government," which by a gross abuse of language they mis-term "the Laos Resistance Government," has been fabricated lock, stock and barrel by the foreign invader (Bernard Fall, *Anatomy of a Crisis*).

The idea that the Communist movement in South Vietnam was a spontaneous and local revolution against the legitimate government of that country, un-guided and un-supported by North Vietnam until the United States weighed in in the early 1960s, is just silly. The idea that Ho Chi Minh became an aggressive Communist hegemonic egomaniac because he was spurned by the West is even sillier. North Vietnam had its Communist fangs into Laos, Cambodia, and South Vietnam since the 1950s, and they had no intention of letting go.

The North Vietnamese occupied whole swathes of the eastern Laotian border to build and secure what became known as the Ho Chi Minh Trail and dropped paratroopers into action when the Pathet Lao were driven from Vientiane, the administrative capital of Laos. While the rightist government was restored and was the official government of Laos, the North Vietnamese and Pathet Lao divided the country virtually in half, de facto annexing eastern Laos to North Vietnam.

For the next thirteen years, a small cadre of CIA operatives, the Hmong army, a few Thai mercenaries, and (later) massive support from American airpower upheld the Kingdom of Laos (with the exception of eastern Laos and the Ho Chi Minh trail). With large portions of the country changing hands frequently, the war in Laos became a violent stalemate, its ultimate fate dependent on the outcome of the war between North and South Vietnam.

That's Some Trail

The Ho Chi Minh Trail was actually a vast network of roads, trails, and tracks, running from North Vietnam down through eastern Laos and Cambodia splitting off into South Vietnam. Constantly upgraded, diverted, and maintained with North Vietnamese and local labor, it was the primary route of North Vietnamese troops, weapons, and supplies throughout the war.

Early in the conflict, in 1962, President Kennedy sought to "send a message" to the Communists (and to Americans who thought his foreign policy was far too timid, especially given its expansive rhetoric and promises). The president ordered the 7th Fleet into the Gulf of Thailand and sent 3,000 American troops to a position just below the Mekong River separating Thailand and Laos. The Marines had with them their transport helicopters, ready to launch toward Vientiane, less than fifty miles away. (Years later these very same helicopters, at that time operated by Air America, a CIA contract enterprise, could be seen in Laos supporting "U.S. Aid" operations. The word "Marines" was clearly visible through the new green paint job. U.S. Aid operations were permitted

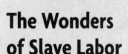

The Wonders of Slave Labor

The Ho Chi Minh Trail, essential to North Vietnam's war strategy, could never have been constructed by emulating the U. S. government's competitive bidding process. Hanoi was fortunate to find 30,000 coolies who were willing to spend the rest of their lives humping through the Laotian jungle while death rained from above, salary not negotiable. Much like the slaves bidding on the "pyramid project" for the Pharaoh Company, coolies in North Vietnam didn't have a lot of leverage.

under the various agreements concerning Laos. Overt military assistance was not.)

Kennedy chided Khrushchev for failing to live up to the Geneva agreement of 1954, and demanded that he cease Soviet operations in Laos in support of the Pathet Lao. Khrushchev replied that the North Vietnamese/Pathet Lao would not again undertake large scale military action in Laos, and asserted that Kennedy should take his Marines out of Thailand. The Marines were withdrawn, and Kennedy instructed his ambassador at large, Averell Harriman, to reach a neutrality settlement with Laos, calling for a coalition government and the withdrawal of all foreign military.

The Russians never intended to live up to their side of the bargain. Although they eventually stopped their direct activity in Laos, they made no effort to stop the North Vietnamese from occupying portions of Laos as they saw fit. Hanoi, in fact, had viewed the settlement in Laos as a potential "template" for a gradual annexation of South Vietnam—support and supply the local Communists, infiltrate North Vietnamese troops, and grind away the opposition while denying any involvement whatsoever. Since it was clear to the government in Hanoi that the United States did not want to commit combat troops to Indochina, they saw no drawback to applying pressure to the Laotian government. Hanoi was confident, of course, that it would dominate any such coalition. The United States, however, wasn't so foolish. American intelligence revealed, unsurprisingly, that Hanoi had no intention of abiding by the agreement in Laos, so the United States never seriously considered a Laotian solution (if one wants to call it that) for South Vietnam—that is, recognizing the Communist terrorists in South Vietnam as a legitimate force to be included in a coalition South Vietnamese government.[4]

By the late 1960s, there were upwards of 40,000 North Vietnamese troops in Laos at any one time. North Vietnamese tanks and anti-aircraft artillery were plentiful in the north and northeast of Laos (the anti-aircraft batteries were thick along the Ho Chi Minh Trail). Laos maintained nominal independence and freedom until the fall of Saigon, when it became a satellite of Communist Vietnam.

A Shared Responsibility

Four United States presidents, two from each party, advocated, supported, and defended the American involvement in the war in Vietnam: Dwight David Eisenhower (who wanted to halt Communist aggression in Asia), John F. Kennedy (who had long supported South Vietnam's independence), Lyndon Johnson (who did not want to be "the first American president to lose a war"), and Richard Nixon (who was elected to conduct the war to an honorable end). Only Nixon came close to delivering what he had promised the American people. The irony is that Nixon, derided by the radical Left as a war-monger, not only had a much more humble and pragmatic foreign policy than Kennedy, but was the president who finally ended the war—only to see a vengeful Democratic Congress throw away the victory he had won in 1973 by refusing to support the South Vietnamese with supplies and air support during the North Vietnamese invasion of 1975.

Still, that was in the future. In 1962, the Geneva agreement created a coalition government, with representation from rightists, neutralists, and Communists. Such an accommodation amidst the Laotian war made Laos a very interesting place. In Vientiane's venerable Hotel Laing Xaing on the north bank of the Mekong, Russians and Chinese often sat table to table with Air America pilots and U.S. embassy and U.S. AID personnel. In the Royal capital of Luang Prabang, Pathet Lao guerrillas would shop for meat and vegetables in the morning before heading back to the jungle and returning to the war. Everyone seemed to realize that the real war was in South Vietnam (with the Viet Cong stepping up its terrorist tactics almost daily), and that its outcome would dictate the future for both sides.

Vietnam: JFK's godchild

It was no surprise to Kennedy watchers that when the president decided to draw the line in the sand against Communist aggression, he drew it along the DMZ of a country thousands of miles away, across the Pacific Ocean. Maintaining the independence of South Vietnam had been a priority of Kennedy's from his days as a young senator from Massachusetts. In 1956, Kennedy declared, "Vietnam represents the cornerstone of the Free World in Southeast Asia, the keystone to the arch, the finger in the dike. Burma, Thailand, India, Japan, the Philippines, and obviously Laos and Cambodia are among those whose security would be threatened if the red tide of Communism overflowed into Vietnam."[5] Kennedy underlined the point by saying that Vietnam was the "proving ground for democracy in Asia." We were "the godparents" to "little Vietnam."[6] Kennedy's defense of Vietnam was part and parcel of a litany of influences on Kennedy: his Navy service in the Pacific in World War II, the foreign policy consensus that America was a Pacific power (and the guardian of Japan, the Philippines, Taiwan, and South Korea), his Cold

A Noble Cause

Were the citizens of South Vietnam worth the effort we made to defend them? Of course they were. They were certainly no less worthy than the South Koreans we had defended—and defend to this day. Hundreds of thousands of South Vietnamese young men fought in the war—and more than 200,000 South Vietnamese young men gave their lives defending their country. Millions of South Vietnamese families risked their lives and livelihoods by standing up against the terrorism of the Viet Cong. The hundreds of thousands of "boat people" fleeing the Communists after the fall of Saigon should be testimony enough to the willingness of the people of South Vietnam to bear hardship in order to secure their freedom; and the estimated one million South Vietnamese who were forced into reeducation programs (in which more than 150,000 died) should be reminder enough of what we were fighting to prevent.

War anti-Communism, his Catholicism, and his desire to embody a forceful foreign policy; he was, after all, the author of the anti-appeasement tome (his senior thesis at Harvard in 1940), *Why England Slept*. And he had something to prove.

Kennedy had campaigned on the existence of an alleged missile gap between the United States and the Soviet Union. He had promised to lead the fight for freedom abroad. Yet his administration came out of the gate looking like it was led by Adlai Stevenson (a wishy-washy liberal) rather than by a virile young war hero, lover of James Bond novels, and sponsor of the Green Berets, and Kennedy was well aware of it. But there was something else in the makeup of the Kennedy administration that would sow the seeds of disaster: it was an administration of the self-styled "best and brightest" (as David Halberstam later called them), and in its hubris it thought it knew, and Secretary of Defense Robert McNamara thought he could quantify, everything. Included in this omni-competence was the belief that it knew better than Diem how to govern South Vietnam.

In South Vietnam, through the end of the 1950s and into the first years of the 1960s, Diem's government held a tenuous advantage over the Communists. Even Hanoi acknowledged that the South was making headway in destroying the Communist insurgency. Although there were ebbs and flows in the battles, the Viet Cong, as the Communist guerrillas were now called, had won no significant victories against Diem's military. However, the Communists still held vast areas of the country hostage, North Vietnam's ever-increasing support for the Viet Cong was being felt by 1961, and there was little confidence that the ARVN (Army of the Republic of Vietnam) were any sort of match for the NVA (the North Vietnamese Army). The ARVN were improving, but their resources, airpower, and mobile artillery, were still limited; worse, they had none of the ideological fanaticism of the Communists, and more of an interest in survival than victory. Yet, despite all this, South Vietnam was muddling through.

Diem's problem, at least from his perspective, was with his allies. For all the success he felt he had achieved in consolidating his position and keeping the Communists in check, he was bombarded by advice, criticisms, and threats from the United States that he needed to govern more like an American and make broad changes in government policy and appointments to that end. Diem, not unreasonably, thought he knew better how to run his country, especially in a time of war. Even the West, he said repeatedly, recognized that during a wartime crisis, governments sometimes had to limit civil liberties. He felt he was being held to an inappropriate Western standard. He did not want to become an American "protectorate." He wanted to defend South Vietnam's political independence—even if he relied on American aid, which the United States periodically threatened to suspend or cut off.

Not only were American demands often, in Diem's view as the head of state of a sovereign nation, insulting and unreasonable, but the Americans were schizophrenic. At different times Diem would hear, on the one hand (from Ambassador Elbridge Durbrow, our man in Saigon from 1957 to 1961), that "the Republic of South Vietnam would remain under attack from within as long as it failed to take genuine steps toward improving the economic and social welfare of its people."[7] On the other hand, he'd hear from General Samuel Williams, chief of the U.S. Military Assistance Advisory Group, that "economic and political reforms are impossible until the partisan violence has been crushed militarily."[8] Diem's own view inclined to that of General Williams—though he was not about to accept American ideas about reform over his own.

In 1962, Kennedy approved boosts in American military aid to South Vietnam, including helicopters, armored troop carriers, and other special weaponry, plus a significant increase in military advisors. General Paul Harkins was placed in charge of the Military Assistance Command, Vietnam (MACV), replacing the earlier Military Assistance Advisory Group. The change reflected the growing commitment, influence, and operational role of the American military. Harkins was bullish that Kennedy's efforts would reap rewards in Vietnam. His reports in 1962 and 1963 were increasingly upbeat and positive. He sought and obtained a good relationship with Diem. Detractors of Diem and the ARVN accused Harkins of being an armchair general, sitting in his office in Saigon opining about the success of Diem's forces in the countryside. In actuality, Harkins was a good commander, making frequent trips to the countryside and seeking advice and information from American military advisors in the field.

One frustration for Kennedy was that Harkins's reports were offset by others that took a radically different view. Men he considered brilliant and whom he trusted presented him with conflicting information. "How can three people go to Vietnam and see the same situation, talk to the same people, and then come back and give me three different analyses?" he was reported to have asked.[9]

Kennedy maintained his hawkish anti-Communist rhetoric in public, but in the Oval Office he was less sure of what the U.S. mission in Vietnam should be. He was steadfastly against the commitment of American combat troops, but wholeheartedly approved a big escalation in the number of military advisors and the amount of equipment we sent to South Vietnam. He was particularly interested in the new counterinsurgency techniques that were being developed by America's Special Forces, and was a champion of expanding such units. At the same time, he remained skeptical of the Pentagon and annoyed at the lack of consensus among his closest advisors.

The reality on the ground has been reported by Wilfred Burchett, a pro-Communist Australian, who actually lived with the Viet Cong during part of the early 1960s, and spoke with many of their leaders. "In terms of territory and population, Diem made a considerable comeback in 1962." The ARVN "registered a number of successes and held the strategic and tactical initiative. In the final analysis," Burchett stated, "1962 was Diem's year."[10]

JFK's big adventure goes sour

In July 1963, Kennedy appointed Henry Cabot Lodge as the new ambassador to Vietnam. The appointment was widely believed to be political—in the sense that Lodge was a Republican and a possible presidential candidate. By sending him to South Vietnam, Kennedy gave a nod to bipartisanship and got rid of a possible rival. He also made perhaps the worst possible choice to deal with the small, shy, intellectual Diem. Lodge was an arrogant, aristocratic Bostonian. A likely apocryphal story, but one that was widely told because it reflected the underlying reality, was that when Lodge arrived in Saigon, he telephoned Diem and asked him to come by the embassy. Diem replied that *he* was president of the country and that Lodge could come by to see *him.* That was the Lodge-Diem relationship: Lodge arrogating to himself the role of shadow president, and Diem standing on his honor.

Lodge never understood Diem's fear of looking like an American stooge. Lodge badgered and bullied Diem, pressing him to make democratic reforms, never realizing that the one thing that united the Vietnamese was their desire to be free from foreign domination—whether that domination came from French colonialists or American Democrats. If Diem became Lodge's "boy," his credibility with his own people would be shot. The North Vietnamese understood this, which was why Communist propaganda relentlessly portrayed Diem as an American puppet.

For Diem, of course, it was not merely a matter of appearances. He believed that his American allies did not understand South Vietnam and could not overcome their own deeply ingrained assumption that there was no reason why Saigon could not become a tropical San Francisco or St. Louis or Miami. Discussing the Buddhist protests against his regime, Diem told Marguerite Higgins, a reporter from the *New York Herald Tribune,* "I cannot seem to convince the [American] embassy that this is Vietnam—not the United States of America."[11]

Lodge always said that the immediate threat to Diem's regime was not from the Communist North, but from political opposition in the South. What he didn't mean, but what proved to be the case, was that the greatest threat to Diem's regime was the American embassy in Saigon. If anyone was in a position to know this, it was Lodge himself, since he was plotting a campaign to get rid of Diem.

In 1963, Lodge gained two journalistic allies. Neil Sheehan and David Halberstam were two twenty-something journalists (with UPI and the *New York Times,* respectively) who arrived in Vietnam eager for front page stories. They were diligent reporters, arrogant and idealistic, unwilling to take no for an answer or to be excluded from certain information on the grounds of "military security," and they didn't shy away from the action. But like so many brilliant men, their egos took precedence over common sense, or the common good. In their striving to dig up stories of South Vietnamese incompetence and stupidity, they made the already perilous position of South Vietnam and its president even more so. Sheehan and Halberstam's reporting positioned them not as disinterested observers, but as political actors who could influence the fate of the government in Saigon.

Halberstam and Sheehan had befriended, or been befriended by, Colonel John Paul Vann, one of the most outspoken Army advisors in the Southeast Asian theater. Although the young reporters were most likely unaware of it, Vann had a career that most resembled a rap sheet. An unrepentant self-promoter and womanizer, Vann had no chance of becoming a general, because of an allegation of statutory rape of a minor on his record. Nevertheless he was a fearless and a dedicated advisor to the ARVN 7th Division at the time—even if he ended up blackening its reputation and, more important, that of Diem.

Blaming Diem

In January 1963, the ARVN 7th Division, which had been clearing the Mekong Delta of Viet Cong, was ordered to take the village of Bac (American journalists added the prefix "ap," which means hamlet). From intelligence reports, the ARVN expected to find 120 Viet Cong in the village. Instead, there were two times that many Viet Cong in the vicinity—and their positions were well dug in and fortified. Moreover, the VC had been tipped off about ARVN's planned attack.

After the first helicopter-insertion of ARVN troops into the landing zone, fog delayed the next two insertions. The pilots (American) landed the troops too close to the tree line, exposing them to witheringly accurate ground fire. Artillery and air strikes in support of the ARVN were misdirected. The ARVN airborne reserve force was dropped on the wrong side of the village. The "field" that the ARVN were to *rush* across was eighteen inches of sucking mud. The ARVN suffered eighty killed and one hundred wounded. Three American advisors were killed and eight others were wounded. The ARVN troops were inept and lacked aggressiveness. Their battlefield leadership was pitiful. The battle of Ap Bac was a small scale disaster.

John Paul Vann watched it all from an observation aircraft. He had trained these troops. He had even boasted about them. And now they were letting him down, humiliating him, and he was furious. That fury turned a bungled operation, which was not representative of anything greater than itself, into an overblown indictment of Diem.

The People's Choice

Personal weaknesses aside, John Paul Vann was as highly decorated as he was controversial, and he was dedicated to winning the war in Vietnam. He once observed, "The basic fact of life is that the overwhelming majority of the population—somewhere around 95 percent—prefer the government of Vietnam to a Communist government or the government that's being offered by the other side."[12]

Halberstam and Sheehan revered Vann as their "inside" guy in the military, a guy who told them the *real* truth about operations, and he had a heck of a story for them about Ap Bac. In Vann's telling, Ap Bac was not just a screwed up operation—not exactly unknown in war—but an indictment of Diem's regime. "Diem," he said, "had selected cronies and political friends as generals." That wasn't all. "Diem's generals were told to keep their casualties low because high losses incited a mutinous attitude and could foment a coup." If Halberstam and Sheehan had been the reporters they thought they were, they would have seen through Vann's pique. The idea that the loss of 80 men in a division of 10,000 men would inspire generals to thoughts of disloyalty, let alone a coup, especially when, in Vann's own scenario, the generals were Diem cronies, beggared belief. Vann's analysis also cut against the grain of another common journalistic indictment of the ARVN generals—that they were uncaring brutes who actually relished casualties because battlefield deaths allowed them to collect the pay for troops whose losses weren't reported to Saigon.

The press ridiculed General Harkins at MACV for trying to put a positive spin on Ap Bac. But the fact was, most American military advisors agreed that however badly executed the plan, it represented a significant advance in ARVN capabilities. The battle plan had been a complex, coordinated ground, air, artillery, and airborne operation. Though it hadn't worked, it was still reasonable to expect that the ARVN's performance would improve with experience.

Ap Bac was a small engagement, but it created an enduring template into which much later reporting of the war was trimmed to fit: the government in Saigon was corrupt, and the ARVN were next to worthless. It was also perfect fodder for Henry Cabot Lodge's campaign against Diem.

Flaming Buddhists

One of the enduring images of the Vietnam war is of an elderly Buddhist monk who set himself aflame in protest against the Diem government in 1963. The "burning monk" (Thich Quang Duc) became the symbol of a government allegedly unworthy of American support.

Long before the "barbeque" of Thich Quang Duc, as Madame Nhu (the "evil brother's" wife) callously and foolishly called it (adding fuel to the fire, so to speak), Diem had been plagued by trouble with the Buddhists. It wasn't that Diem was anti-Buddhist. He certainly wasn't. Diem's vice president was a Buddhist (who told a group of foreign diplomats that the regime should "crush the Buddhist movement [against Diem] without pity"[13]), as was his Minister of Foreign Affairs. His eighteen member cabinet consisted of five Catholics, five Confucians, and eight Buddhists. Of the thirty-eight province chiefs, twelve were Catholic and twenty-six were either Buddhists or Confucians. Some of his leading generals were Buddhist as well.

So while Diem was not anti-Buddhist, the radicalized Buddhists of Saigon and Hue were certainly anti-Diem. Less often reported, but well-documented, is that these radical anti-Diem Buddhists were heavily penetrated by the Communists. Thich Tri Quang, the most prominent of the radical Buddhist leaders, was never proven to be a Communist agent himself, though he was born in the north, had served with the Viet Minh, and had a brother who was a senior official in Hanoi's Ministry of the Interior. What has been proven is that the Communists infiltrated the Buddhist movement, as well as groups who supported the radical Buddhists. If nothing else, the Communists and the radical Buddhists shared a few common goals: they wanted the Americans gone (because the Buddhists thought the departure of the big, hairy foreigners would "give peace a chance"), and they wanted Diem gone.[14]

The Buddhists objected to Diem because they saw him as an obstacle to peace (even though the "peace" that came from the Communists meant religious persecution for the Buddhists), but also because of parochial issues: they believed that his administration was anti-Buddhist. It is true that the South Vietnamese government was top-heavy with Catholic appointees in relation to their percentage of the population. But this had more to do with the preference the French colonists had shown for the Catholic population than with any prejudice on Diem's part. Catholic Vietnamese were, in general, the best educated segment of the population and the segment with the most experience in government.

Moreover, contrary to the impression left by many journalists, South Vietnam was not strictly a "Buddhist" country. In a country of fifteen to sixteen million people, probably no more than three or four million considered Buddhism their religion. Another four million were Confucians. One and a half million were Catholic. The rest of the country belonged to such exotic sects as the Cao Dai and Hoa Hao, or were animists, Taoists,

Protestant Christians, Hindus, or Muslims. A strong and visible concentration of Buddhists in Saigon gave rise to the impression that South Vietnam was strongly or solely Buddhist. No more than a handful of Buddhist temples out of thousands saw demonstrations against the South Vietnamese government.

The flashpoint, so to speak, in the radical Buddhist versus Diem conflict came in May 1963, when thousands of Buddhists gathered in Hue to celebrate the 2,527th birthday of Buddha. The week before, during the celebration of Archbishop Ngo Dinh Thuc's (Diem's brother) twenty-fifth anniversary of his ordination, the celebrants flew papal flags. For the

The Missing Picture

There are several iconic pictures of the Vietnam War. One is of the Saigon police chief executing a Viet Cong prisoner during the Tet Offensive. Missing from this picture of apparent police brutality is that the VC prisoner had been captured after the Viet Cong had beheaded a Vietnamese colonel and killed his wife and six children. The photographer, Eddie Adams, later said he regretted that the photo had been so widely used to accuse the police chief of brutality.

Another horribly memorable picture is of a naked young Vietnamese girl fleeing a napalm attack on her village. Used as a symbol of the brutality and terror of war and its impact on the people of Vietnam, it stands well. But how many of us remember that the photo was taken after U.S. troops had left Vietnam, or that the napalm was dropped by a South Vietnamese pilot who was attacking the foreign troops who had invaded the young girl's village? How many Americans felt rage then, or feel it now, at the invading North Vietnamese who had driven the girl and her family from their home?

Buddhists' celebration, however, the deputy province chief, a Catholic, tried to enforce an old decree prohibiting religious flags from being publicly displayed. Legally, only the national flag of South Vietnam could be flown from any church, pagoda, or other place of religious worship. In Vietnam, flags were enormously potent symbols, rousing even stronger feeling (much) than the stars and stripes do for ardent American patriots, which is why their use was circumscribed by government edict.

But in this case, of course, the 1958 law on flag-flying appeared to have been applied inconsistently (though the province chief's defenders argued that he had reasserted the law *because* it had been violated during the Catholic celebrations), and the already aggrieved Buddhists now felt even more so. Protests and Buddhist flag-waving erupted in Hue, followed by what might be described as a riot. In the confusion of trying to break up the protestors, shots were fired and nine protestors were killed. The actual details of the incident are contested: the Buddhists said they were fired upon in cold blood; the government argued that its troops had first used fire hoses, then blanks, then shots in the air to disperse the crowd, and only opened fire after a VC agitator set off an explosion (or fired off the first shots).

What is not contested is that two days after the incident, the provincial chief publicly apologized to the Buddhists, thousands of whom had gathered to protest the shooting, expressed sorrow for those who were killed, and promised that the government would provide compensation to their families. The American consul in Hue, seeing the event, cabled the embassy, "Believe crisis nearing end."

Never to be mollified, Thich Tri Quang and other militant Buddhist leaders demanded punishment of the officials involved in the incident, removal of all restrictions on the display of flags, and *a prohibition against the arrest of Buddhists involved in protests.* The Buddhist militants didn't expect or want reconciliation. They wanted Diem gone and believed they could wage a propaganda war to that end.

The government issued a communiqué in late May that reaffirmed constitutional protections of religious freedom and firmly forswore discrimination. It had no effect. Throughout the summer protests continued. Some were peaceful; some were broken up with tear gas, clubs, and arrests. The government replaced its top officials in Hue in early June, but that also failed to pacify the angry Buddhists.

On June 11, 1963, Diem's battle with the militant Buddhists escalated out of control. Near the Xa Lao pagoda in Saigon, a sedan stopped and an elderly monk and two younger monks got out. The older monk seated himself on a pillow in the street while his associates doused him with gasoline. The monk, Quang Duc, calmly struck a match and set himself on fire. With loud speakers in hand, activist monks told the gathered crowd, in English and Vietnamese, that Quang Duc was dying to protest Diem's treatment of the Buddhists and refusal to meet their demands.

Diem did reach a tentative agreement with some of the Buddhist leaders: in return for ceasing all demonstrations, the government would remove all uniformed government personnel from Buddhist pagodas, agree to let Buddhists fly religious flags outside their pagodas on holidays, and punish officials who interfered with Buddhist religious activities. But no press release of the actual agreement between Diem and the Buddhists (announced in a communiqué released June 16) could possibly approach the impact of the photos of the burning monk, taken by Malcolm Browne and published around the world, often with this caption: "This Buddhist priest, the Reverend Quang Duc, has just set himself on fire. He dies to protest South Vietnam's religious persecution of Buddhists (70% of population)." It was brilliant propaganda. For many Americans, their first introduction to our involvement in Vietnam began with the question, "What kind of people are we supporting over there? How bad must a government be if people burn themselves to death in the street?" Quick to answer were correspondents like David Halberstam, who loathed Diem and wrote pieces vilifying his regime. Halberstam's idealistic view of how Diem should govern, and his obvious disdain for foreign journalists (who he sometimes felt were the cause of his problems with the United States) prejudiced him to the point that even President Kennedy lodged a mild rebuke with the *New York Times* at one point.

In his struggle against the militant Buddhists, Diem had a dubious ally in the person of his brother and chief political advisor, Ngo Dinh Nhu. While Diem alternated between being dismissive of Buddhist complaints—saying they were demanding rights they already had—and trying to appease his opponents, Nhu and his wife took a harder line—and one that made for good copy. Madame Nhu's comments about the "barbequing" and

An Uncontrollable Puppet

While President Diem's enemies routinely accused him of being America's puppet, the U.S. State Department was furious that Diem wouldn't follow orders, directions, or recommendations. In a similar irony, Diem was repeatedly castigated by his Western critics for not delegating enough authority, though these very same critics criticized the rest of the South Vietnamese government as incompetent. Diem's job might be described as trying to memorize the U.S. Tax Code while dancing in a cobra pit with your hair on fire. The Viet Cong were terrorizing the countryside, the Buddhists were revolting, the intelligentsia didn't like him, there was mutinous talk in the Army, and the Americans were demanding that he act like an American or step down—except for those Americans (including the *New York Times*) who told him what a fine job he was doing. Diem took no orders but his own—which might be why his alleged puppet master, John F. Kennedy, assented to his removal if not his assassination.

"let them burn and we shall clap our hands," and her husband's addition that he would gladly supply the gasoline for more such barbecues, received greater press coverage and attention than Diem's attempts to settle the disputes.

Meanwhile, militant Buddhist mobs continued to foment dissent against Diem. They threw rocks at the police, knowing the reaction would be swift and newsworthy. More monks lit themselves up in towns where there had not been any repression by the government. On August 18, some 20,000 protesters massed around the Xa Loi pagoda, the largest in Saigon, with militant monks calling for the overthrow of Diem's government. Diem declined to have the mob broken up, showing the restraint he had promised to American Ambassador Frederick Nolting (who had not yet been replaced by Henry Cabot Lodge). But it bought him little credit with his American critics, and it prompted many in South Vietnam's government, among them his brother Nhu, to think Diem was too soft.

On August 21, 1963, under cover of darkness, Vietnamese police and Special Forces, answering to Nhu, launched a series of raids against Buddhist pagodas, making hundreds of arrests and injuring thousands. Nhu struck during the interval when American ambassador Frederick Nolting was making way for Henry Cabot Lodge. Nolting had told Lodge that Diem had agreed to do everything he could to pacify the Buddhists. Nolting felt betrayed and foolish, given Nhu's crackdown, and Lodge came to Saigon considering Diem a liar. In his first report from South Vietnam, Lodge passed along comments from Vietnamese generals and government officials calling for Nhu's removal from Diem's government.

The end of Diem

The coup chatter among Saigon's generals escalated. Diem had already survived two attempted coups, one in 1960 and one in 1962, when his palace was bombed by mutinous Vietnamese air force officers. Few

ARVN generals were repulsed by Nhu's attacks against the Buddhist militants. What worried them was America's reaction. At the beginning of the Buddhist crisis, the United States had threatened to cut off aid to South Vietnam. The ARVN generals knew that Diem was unpopular with the U.S. State Department. They knew the American press had turned against Diem. All of this emboldened them and, in their own eyes, justified their conspiracies.

David Halberstam was reporting for the *New York Times* that Diem was both brutal and finished as a political figure in South Vietnam. According to Halberstam, thirty monks had been killed by the government in Hue. This led to the dispatch of a United Nations investigation team. When the team arrived, the thirty monks had shrunk to four, and, amazingly, those four consented to interviews with the UN investigators.[15]

Still, Halberstam continued his attack on Diem. The focus of his "news" reports was that Diem had lost almost all support of his people, that he was "no longer a serious political figure," and that "key Vietnamese have long waited for Washington to give an indication that it has had enough of the Ngo family." Clearly there were those in the South Vietnamese government who wanted Diem ousted. But equally as clear was that Halberstam's interest in making news (influencing American policy) was as strong as his desire to report it, and he had the willing ears of the anti-Diemists in Washington.

On the Saturday morning following the assault on the pagodas (thirty pagodas out of five thousand in the country), four men, Averell Harriman (undersecretary of state for political affairs), Roger Hilsman (assistant secretary of state for far eastern affairs), George Ball (undersecretary of state), and Michael Forrestal (on the senior staff of the national security council), drafted a memo to Ambassador Lodge which began the final chapter in Diem's presidency, and his life. The key words of the cable were: "The US Government cannot tolerate situation in which power lies in Nhu's hands. Diem must be given chance to rid himself of Nhu and his coterie.... If, in spite of all your efforts, Diem remains obdurate and refuses, then we must face the possibility that Diem himself cannot be preserved...." The Vietnamese generals were to be advised that continued economic and military support would be impossible unless Nhu was removed, and that if Diem refused, the United States would no longer support him.[16]

Kennedy gave his consent to the cable, provided it was first approved by Secretary of State Dean Rusk and Defense Secretary Robert McNamara. McNamara never saw the cable. Neither did John McCone, head of the CIA. Chairman of the Joint Chiefs of Staff General Maxwell Taylor was given only a summary while he was at a restaurant. The cable was sent that evening without McNamara's, McCone's, or Taylor's approval. In the president's office on Monday, McCone, McNamara, and General Taylor, all of whom supported Diem, were furious. In his personal journal Kennedy conceded: "The wire was badly drafted. It should have never been sent on a Saturday. I should not have given my consent to it without a roundtable conference at which McNamara and Taylor could have presented their views."

In the meeting with McCone, McNamara, and Taylor, Kennedy let his own anger boil over (perhaps because he suddenly found himself responsible for a possible coup to which he was not fully committed). He railed at the role Halberstam was playing in Vietnam. He even suggested that the cable had been inspired by the *New York Times*. "Halberstam is actually running a political campaign," Kennedy told McCone, McNamara, and Taylor. "He is wholly unobjective, reminiscent of [*New York Times* reporter Herbert] Matthews in the Castro days. It is essential that we do not permit Halberstam unduly to influence our actions."[17]

Nevertheless, the cable went into effect immediately. Lodge directed the CIA to make contact with the ARVN generals. The CIA's Lucien "Lou" Conein, a colorful old Vietnam hand (he'd been dropped into Vietnam by the OSS in 1945 to fight the Japanese and sent back to Vietnam in the 1950s by the CIA), spoke to ARVN Chief of Staff General Tran Thien

Khiem. Khiem was not an enthusiast for a coup. He knew that Diem and Nhu were inseparable so that a demand to get rid of Nhu or else meant "or else"—and if that were the case, he did not know anyone, civilian or military, who could fill Diem's shoes as a politician and national leader. Still, Khiem said he would talk to the generals. After he did, he said a coup would be launched within a week.

But it didn't happen; the generals backed down because they believed that a large majority (perhaps two to one) of the troops in Saigon and in its vicinity were loyal to Diem. The political momentum, however, was still against the Diem regime. The cable Lodge sent Washington on August 29, 1963, was clear: "We are launched on a course from which there is no respectable turning back: the overthrow of the Diem government."

Kennedy continued to vacillate over the next month, often sending conflicting signals to Lodge within days of one another. In early September he sent another fact-finding team to Vietnam, composed of General Victor Krulak (McNamara's choice) and Joseph Mendenhall of the State Department (picked by Harriman and Hilsman). Krulak traveled throughout the country talking to dozens of American advisors and South Vietnamese officers. His conclusion: the war was going fairly well and the ARVN had no desire to see Diem removed. Mendenhall spent his time in three South Vietnamese cities. He spoke to Vietnamese civil servants, U.S. State Department officials, and others. His conclusion: if Nhu was left in power, South Vietnam would fall into a religious civil war, or, failing that, to the Viet Cong.

Their reports were given to Kennedy and the National Security Council on September 10, 1963. It was at this meeting that Kennedy quipped, "The two of you did visit the same country, didn't you?"[18] Kennedy's preferred decision was indecision, but under constant pressure from Lodge, he finally ordered that American aid to Diem's government be reduced. The ARVN generals took note, and by mid-October a coup was back in the works. Anti-Diem reporters fed the fire. Neil Sheehan (UPI) wrote:

"The Diem government's war against the Viet Cong rebels cannot be won unless the Diem regime is replaced with a more liberal group that can win the support of the whole population"[19] (a statement of political desire, not the facts on the ground, as Victor Krulak had established). Stanley Karnow wrote in the *Saturday Evening Post*: "No matter how much the United States supports the un-popular regime of Ngo Dinh Diem, this regime's chances of victory over the Communists are just about nil."[20] In fact, the Diem government was, at that time, winning the war.

The military and the CIA continued to support Diem, leading Lodge to request that the CIA station chief in Saigon, John Richardson, be replaced. Director of Central Intelligence John McCone declined. But then his hand was forced when an anti-Diem journalist "outed" Richardson as the CIA's man in Saigon. After that, Richardson had to be transferred.

Kennedy waffled, trying to find a consensus that didn't exist, and buying time by sending McNamara and Taylor on yet another fact-finding mission in late September. Finally the ARVN generals had had enough— not of Diem, but of American pressure, threats, and aid cuts. The generals agreed to Lodge's entreaties, and a coup was set for the first of November. With the overthrow of Diem now a *fait accompli*, Kennedy had two concerns. First: that the action not go forward without a very high degree of probable success; second: that the physical well-being of Diem and Nhu be assured. There was never an executive order or memo ordering or even suggesting a coup go forward. The American position was couched in terms of "not stopping a legitimate attempt" to change the government of South Vietnam.

Diem's supporters in the United States made a last ditch to save him. Clare Booth Luce—a Catholic convert and strong anti-Communist, former Republican congresswoman from Connecticut, former ambassador to Italy, and a celebrated writer whose husband Henry Luce happened to own *Time* magazine—took out a full page ad in the *New York Times* defending Diem's government. Marine General Victor Krulak, meanwhile, distributed the report of an eight-member Congressional delegation. It found that Diem was winning the war and had no rivals when it came to political leadership; there was no viable alternative to the current South Vietnamese president. (The congressional delegation also deplored the "arrogant, emotional, unobjective and ill-informed" American press in Vietnam.)

On the morning of November 1, 1963, the coup began. The generals, with General "Big" Minh as their titular head, had planned well, and the coup was executed with a skill that confounded the ARVN at Ap Bac. Diem and Nhu, however, escaped. Hiding in Cholon in the house of a wealthy businessman, Diem contacted the coup leaders and offered to surrender in exchange for safe passage. He received no credible assurances. Diem and Nhu were arrested the next morning as they came out of a Catholic church. They were packed into an armored car, their hands tied behind their backs, and murdered. A gruesome photo of the slain brothers was sent around the world. In Washington, D.C., at a long-standing dinner between friends, William Colby (who had stopped to pray for the Diem brothers in the morning), Ambassador Nolting, and John Richardson shook their heads mournfully, wondering how the Kennedy administration could have consented to such a self-defeating act: an act that not only removed the only credible leader of South Vietnam, but that established a precedent for political turmoil far beyond the protests of the Buddhists.

The North Vietnamese politburo had this to say: "Diem was one of the strongest individuals resisting the people and Communism.... Among the anti-Communists in South Vietnam

Not in His Eyes You Aren't

"After all, I am a Chief of State."

—**Ngo Dinh Diem,** pleading with his enemy, American Ambassador Henry Cabot Lodge, for guidance against a coup attempt, just hours before he was assassinated.[22]

or exiled in other countries, no one has sufficient political assets and abilities to cause the others to obey."

Pro-Communist Australian Wilfred Burchett spent time with the North Vietnamese leaders after the coup. He quoted the North Vietnamese as saying, "Diem was a national leader, and you will never be able to replace him—never." They were right.[21]

President Kennedy was said to turn pale and had to leave the room when told what happened. His administration, aided by an arrogant ambassador and an egotistical young newsman, had just overseen the biggest American foreign policy blunder of the twentieth century.

The Limited War Myth

Although the United States fought a limited war in Vietnam, the North Vietnamese did not. Therein lies the basic stupidity of the strategy put in place by Defense Secretary Robert McNamara and John F. Kennedy's and Lyndon Johnson's "best and brightest." It was based on what we might call the mirror theory. If we did "this," then surely they would do "that," because reasonable men would react reasonably.[23]

But no one who knew anything about the Communists in Indochina should have imagined that they would follow our lead in fighting a limited war, or that they had any intention of abiding by what Presidents Kennedy and Johnson thought was reasonable. To the North Vietnamese, the restraints America put upon herself merely provided additional advantages to the cause of Communist revolution.

After World War II, civilian academics, theorists, economists, and other social scientists, most of whom had limited or non-existent experience in combat or planning military strategy, believed that the advent of nuclear weapons had changed the face of war. From that belief grew the doctrine of "limited war," the idea that America could parse its military strength, applying

just the right amount of firepower to convince its adversaries to leave the battlefield or suffer annihilation.

The limited war concept got its first deployment during the Korean War, which some considered a success because the United States accomplished the goal of limiting Communist aggression without resorting to atomic weapons or a vast widening of the conflict. For many others, that war was an exercise in frustration, and set a dangerous precedent of deploying the military with a goal of less than victory.

Robert Osgood, in his *Limited Warfare Revisited*, noted that a defining feature of limited war theory was "gradualism" and the commitment "*not* to apply maximum force toward the military defeat of the adversary; rather it must be to employ force skillfully along a continuous spectrum—from diplomacy, to crises of war, to an overt clash of arms—in order to exert the desired effect on the adversary's will." He goes on: "This principle held an appealing logic for the new breed of United States liberal realists who had discovered the duty of managing power shrewdly in behalf of world order." That very description reeks of the classroom—not of an actual battlefield, not of the actual experience of war, and not of real life.

The troops in Vietnam, few of whom had Ivy League educations, might not have known the theory of gradualism, but they suffered the frustrations and consequences of fighting a "limited war" and knew something was wrong. One of the bloodiest, most brutal battles of the war came in 1969—the battle for Hamburger Hill. The Americans fought their way to the top, then retreated and let the enemy regain the hill. The American soldiers were angry and frustrated. The logic, of course, was that in a war of attrition it makes perfect sense to lure the enemy back to a position of vulnerability (though in this case, the enemy position had been heavily fortified) so that more can be destroyed. The fallacy of that argument was that a war of attrition was not even a remotely effective strategy against the North Vietnamese. And after five long years of combat, even an illiterate American soldier would have known it.

The Kennedy administration "whiz kids" who set America's strategy in the Kennedy and Johnson years believed in applying business models to war. Defense Secretary Robert McNamara had

continued on p. 60

continued from p. 59

been a "whiz kid" at Ford, where he rose to become president of the company, before he joined the Kennedy Administration. He and his colleagues believed in complex statistical analysis, in a managerial approach to war, and in applying the tools of corporate bureaucracy to the military.

The military men, for the most part, believed that violence was violence and was best applied quickly and decisively. As Napoleon said, war was so horrible that it should be carried out with as much violence as possible so as to end it quickly. The "whiz kids" of the Kennedy administration could not have agreed less. The mutual mistrust and, often, contempt led to confusion in the American government about the Vietnam War from its very beginning. JFK was torn between the advice of his own kind—the "whiz kids"—and of military men like Air Force general Curtis LeMay, who took a drastically different view of things. In both Laos and Vietnam, Kennedy's style was aggressive appeasement. In Laos, Kennedy ceded the eastern part of the country to the Communists. This avoided a showdown with the Russians, but it enabled the North Vietnamese to expand the Ho Chi Minh Trail. In Vietnam, Kennedy's "firm stand against Communist aggression" took the form of a few thousand advisors. His lack of a clear, firm policy later led to the largest American blunder of the Vietnam War, the acquiescence to the coup against the only viable national leader in South Vietnam, Ngo Dinh Diem. America, after Kennedy's assassination, was left with a moral commitment to a people whose leader we had allowed to be killed, and a policy of limited war against an intractable and rabid enemy.

Lyndon Johnson inherited Kennedy's mess and failed to clean it up. His mistake, he later admitted, was not to have fired holdovers from the Kennedy administration (with the exception, he said, of Secretary of State Dean Rusk), and not to have trusted his military advisors, preferring to micromanage the war to the point of approving every bombing site and the payload of the bombers. Johnson accepted the strategy of limited war, though he vastly increased the number of troops committed to the battlefield. Military decisions were overseen by civilians who kept one eye on LBJ's top priority, his hugely expansive domestic programs, and the other on the electorate, about which they grew increasingly fearful as the anti-war protests heated up.

Of course, when President Nixon took over, liberals in Congress, academia, and the press lost all restraint in protesting every presumed American "escalation" of the war; a war that many of them suddenly condemned, though it was their own handiwork. The irony is that Nixon fought a limited war far more successfully than its architects had: drawing down American troops, and securing a Korean-style peace for South Vietnam.

It is often said by the war's critics that the problem with the limited war strategy was that the United States military did not know how to fight a guerrilla war. The truth is quite the opposite. The United States had essentially eliminated the Viet Cong, the "guerrillas," after the 1968 Tet Offensive. The general "kill ratio" of American battlefield killed-in-action to enemy battlefield killed-in-action over the course of the war was more than 10 to 1. In some units (the Studies and Observations Group, for example) the ratio was more like 30 to 1. The United States suffered nearly 60,000 dead in Vietnam, but inflicted losses of well over a million enemy dead (more than 1,177,000 by most estimates). Given the war of attrition to which it was committed, the United States military succeeded spectacularly. Given its mission to eliminate the Viet Cong, it succeeded. Given its mission to hurl back the North Vietnamese and defend the integrity of South Vietnam, it succeeded. All of which is to underline that the fault of limited war was not with the United States military forced to fight under its constraints, but with the strategy itself, which utterly failed to end North Vietnam's commitment to conquer Indochina.

Chapter Three

LBJ'S WAR

The immediate consequence of America's dithering, half-hearted acquiescence to the demise of the Diem government was increased instability throughout South Vietnam. Over the next few years (1963 to 1965), there were nine different governments. Plotting and executing coups seemed to be the primary activity of the South Vietnamese officer corps. Well intentioned, justified by circumstances, or sheer power grab (and most coups managed to be all of the above), the atmosphere in Saigon was uncertain and anything but conducive to the successful prosecution of a war which had been going on since 1954, long before the Americans began sending military advisors. Not only did this allow the Communists to regain ground they had lost to Diem, but it created a vacuum in overall leadership and guidance of the war. That vacuum would be filled not by a South Vietnamese president, but by a figure more commanding and secure: General William C. Westmoreland of the United States Army. In June 1964 he became supreme military commander in South Vietnam. Although the massive deployment of American soldiers would not take place for another year, the U.S. had over 15,000 military advisors in country and were beginning to "take charge" of the operations against the Communist forces.

Even before "Westy" took command, the United States military was helping South Vietnam take action against the Communist North (and

Guess what?

‡ "Whiz kid" Robert McNamara thought South Vietnam's western border could be secured with an electric fence

‡ President Lyndon Johnson thought he could dominate and cajole Ho Chi Minh the way he dominated and cajoled American congressmen

‡ North Vietnam's Tet Offensive, which virtually eliminated the Communist Viet Cong, was misreported as a calamitous American defeat

hoping to raise South Vietnamese morale in the process). Together they created OPLAN 34A, a series of clandestine actions to be taken against North Vietnam, including commando raids and sabotage. They were to be carried out exclusively by South Vietnamese personnel, mostly against

What Would U. S. Grant Do?

Admiral Ulysses S. Grant Sharp, who was the Commander in Chief of the United States Pacific Command during the beginning of the Vietnam War, was an outspoken critic of the way the Vietnam War was fought. He believed that the Johnson administration's pinprick bombing attacks needlessly prolonged the war (and led to more American casualties) and that massive bombing of North Vietnam would compel the Communists to surrender (the 1972 Christmas bombing of North Vietnam seemed to prove him right, though Grant was by then retired). A hero of World War II and Korea, Admiral Sharp had no love lost for Defense Secretary Robert McNamara, his civilian analysts in the Pentagon, or their strategy of carefully gradated bombing that would, allegedly, through some scientific formula, push the North Vietnamese to negotiate a settlement. That strategy, he claimed, only negated the effect of bombing, as the enemy found ways to work around such a calibrated use of force. To be effective, bombing had to be massive, with the aim of compelling the enemy to surrender. Like Napoleon, Admiral Sharp believed that the horror of war necessitated using all means at hand to bring it to an end as quickly as possible. "The lesson is that we should never commit the armed forces of the United States to combat unless we have decided at the same time to use the nonnuclear power we have available to win in the shortest possible time."

military installations along the southern coast of North Vietnam. Concurrently, the U.S. Navy began sea patrols in the Tonkin Gulf.

Some believed this show of determination, as slight as it was, would convince the North Vietnamese that the United States was serious about defending South Vietnam. They were obviously wrong about that. Also wrong are those who argue that the United States intended to provoke North Vietnam into an attack that would justify bringing in direct American firepower. America certainly did escalate its commitment to Saigon, after a minor incident in the Tonkin Gulf in August 1964, (which became one of the most celebrated "enemy engagements" of the coming war), but there was no "intent" about it; it just happened.

On August 2, 1964, North Vietnamese torpedo boats attacked the American destroyer USS *Maddox* in international waters in the Gulf of Tonkin. Two days later, August 4, another attack was initially reported, though it is now clear that the USS *Maddox* and USS *C. Turner Joy* misread their sonar data, believed they were under torpedo attack when in fact they weren't, and responded with a barrage that hit nothing but water. In response to the first and suspected second attacks, Admiral U.S. Grant Sharp, Commander in Chief of the Pacific, requested that he be allowed to retaliate against North Vietnam. President Johnson agreed, ordering retaliatory strikes by the 7th Fleet naval forces. On August 5, 1964, aircraft from the carriers USS *Ticonderoga* and USS *Constellation* destroyed an oil storage facility at Vinh and damaged or sank about thirty North Vietnamese patrol boats in port or along the coast.

Of greater significance than the retaliatory strikes was the United States Congress's overwhelming passage of the Tonkin Gulf Resolution on August 7, which authorized President Johnson to employ military force

Books the Viet Cong Wouldn't Want You to Read

Strategy for Defeat: Vietnam in Retrospect, by Admiral U. S. G. Sharp (Presidio Press, 1979).

as he saw fit against the Vietnamese Communists. Congress did not pass the resolution in a burst of passion. The bill actually reflected the bipartisan foreign policy consensus—true since the time of President Harry Truman—that Communist aggression had to be contained; and Congress was well aware that Vietnam was the flashpoint of Southeast Asia. Senator William Fulbright, Chairman of the Senate Foreign Relations Committee, in answer to a question during the floor debate, agreed that such a resolution would authorize the president to "use such force as could lead to

The Tonkin Gulf Resolution

88TH UNITED STATES CONGRESS
Joint Resolution

To promote the maintenance of international peace and security in southeast Asia.

Whereas naval units of the Communist regime in Vietnam, in violation of the principles of the Charter of the United Nations and of international law, have deliberately and repeatedly attacked United States naval vessels lawfully present in international waters, and have thereby created a serious threat to international peace; and

Whereas these attacks are part of a deliberate and systematic campaign of aggression that the Communist regime in North Vietnam has been waging against its neighbors and the nations joined with them in the collective defense of their freedom; and

Whereas the United States is assisting the peoples of southeast Asia to protect their freedom and has no territorial, military or political ambitions in that area, but desires only that these peoples should be left in peace to work out their own destinies in their own way: Now, therefore, be it

war."[1] If one wants to date the Vietnam War from the Tonkin Gulf Resolution, it has to be said that the Congress knew exactly what it was doing.

Any claim that the United States would not have entered into the Vietnam War if President Johnson or the military had not "fabricated" the second North Vietnamese attack on the USS *Maddox* is spurious. North Vietnam's aggression was plain, and so was our desire to defend an independent South Vietnam. For almost ten years the Communists had been systematically attacking South Vietnamese cities and assassinating village

Resolved by the Senate and House of Representatives of the United States of America in Congress assembled. That the Congress approves and supports the determination of the President, as Commander in Chief, to take all necessary measures to repel any armed attack against the forces of the United States and to prevent further aggression.

Sec. 2.

The United States regards as vital to its national interest and to world peace the maintenance of international peace and security in southeast Asia. Consonant with the Constitution of the United States and the Charter of the United Nations and in accordance with its obligations under the Southeast Asia Collective Defense Treaty, the United States is, therefore, prepared, as the President determines, to take all necessary steps, including the use of armed force, to assist any member or protocol state of the Southeast Asia Collective Defense Treaty requesting assistance in defense of its freedom.

Sec. 3.

This resolution shall expire when the President shall determine that the peace and security of the area is reasonably assured by international conditions created by action of the United Nations or otherwise, except that it may be terminated earlier by concurrent resolution of the Congress.

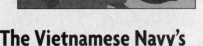

The Vietnamese Navy's First Victory...Which Never Happened?

After the war, General Giap told former Secretary of Defense Robert McNamara that there had been no second attack on American ships in the Gulf of Tonkin. Nevertheless, the North Vietnamese Navy celebrates its anniversary or "tradition day" on 5 August, commemorating the disputed second attack as the day when, as the North Vietnamese put it, "one of our torpedo squadrons chased the USS *Maddox* from our coastal waters, our first victory over the U.S. Navy."[2]

officials. In 1959, Hanoi openly admitted they were supporting the fighting in the South and were sending troops to conquer South Vietnam. Communist actions were exactly why SEATO came into being. The Tonkin Resolution did not begin an American commitment to South Vietnam, it only expanded the commitment that President Kennedy (and before him, President Eisenhower) had made. Nor did the United States go to war against North Vietnam because of the attack in the Tonkin Gulf. The United States went to war because North Vietnam was waging war against South Vietnam.

Shortly after General Westmoreland took command of American forces in Vietnam, the Tonkin Gulf Resolution gave a clear mandate for the president, with the overwhelming support of Congress, to "take all necessary steps, including the use of armed force, to assist any member or protocol member of the Southeast Asia Collective Defense Treaty requesting assistance in defense of its freedom."[3] The mission was not ambiguous; how to achieve it, though, was. The State Department continued to believe that the primary objective was stabilizing the South Vietnamese government; without political stability, the war in the countryside could not be won. Westmoreland and his commanders tended to the opposite view—that if (in the vernacular) you have the enemy by the gonads, their hearts and minds will follow; or, to put it more elegantly, the government of South Vietnam would stabilize once the Communist insurgency and North Vietnamese aggression was halted.

Westmoreland was a soldier's soldier. He came from a family with a long military pedigree, was a graduate of West Point, and had been talent-scouted early on as a fast-rising artillery officer. But Westmoreland's heart and career rested not in the artillery but in the U.S. Army Airborne. His service under General Maxwell Taylor, who commanded the 82nd Airborne in Sicily in World War II, probably got him the job in Vietnam. General Taylor was the United States ambassador to South Vietnam when President Johnson selected Westmoreland for command. With stern, sober, hawk-like features and manner, he was an easy target for later anti-war protesters, who could depict him as a "square" who was too rigid and stupid to understand the alleged moral complexities of the war. In fact, Westmoreland had been promoted to become the youngest major general in the Army in the 1950s, had graduated not only from West Point but from the Harvard Business School, and certainly showed a more acute morality in his service to his country and his defense of the people of South Vietnam than his non-serving critics did who waved Viet Cong flags and cheered on the Communists.

From his appointment as the supreme American commander in Vietnam in 1964 until the Tet Offensive of 1968, Westmoreland pursued his strategy of seeking and destroying the enemy. To his detractors, and there were many by the time he left Vietnam, his vision was based on the concept of "fighting the Russian Army on the plains of Germany,"[4] a war of attrition whereby you overcome the enemy's ability to put troops in the field by simply destroying them. In Vietnam, the concept was flawed for three fundamental reasons:

1. Hanoi was not vulnerable to defeat by attrition, because the Communists were willing to fight to the last North Vietnamese soldier. The Communist government had no constituency to answer to, no voters to tire of the conflict, and no burdensome concern about the "sanctity of life."

2. The Communists in Vietnam had sanctuaries in Laos and Cambodia which were off-limits to U.S. firepower, where they could escape, rebuild their units, and supply themselves with arms and materiel. As long as their Soviet and Chinese backers kept the taps running, the North Vietnamese had no danger of ever running out of supplies.

3. By definition, relying on "Search and Destroy" missions destabilized the entire country. As the Communists could choose the arena for battle, there were few, if any, safe zones in the country for much of 1964 to 1968. Every village, rice field, or back-breakingly constructed bridge, road, or dam was thus put at risk.

Westmoreland recognized some of the shortcomings of his strategy but believed it was the only viable alternative to pursue given the constraints put upon him by the Johnson administration. He believed a counter-insurgency campaign would take too long; he believed that there was no stomach in Washington for anything like MacArthur's aggressive and expansive strategy in the Korean War; and he believed that enemy attrition was what the bean-counters in McNamara's Pentagon understood (as a Harvard Business grad, such quantitative analysis suited Westmoreland, too).

Many officers disagreed with him—especially those who were Marines. One of the ironies of the war is that the knuckle-draggers had a much better understanding of what needed to be done than the military intellectuals did. McNamara and his "whiz kids" were next to clueless. They thought they could secure South Vietnam's western borders with an electric fence.[5] (No kidding.) Your average Marine Corps Gunny Sergeant knew far more what to do than just about everyone in the Kennedy and Johnson administrations did.

The Marines, who had plenty of experience in guerrilla warfare, were proponents of a so-called "ink blot strategy" (this was the phrase used by Marine general Victor Krulak), which aimed to secure South Vietnam village by village. The Marines were inclined to combine the ink-blot strategy with the sort of strategic bombing of North Vietnam recommended by Admiral U. S. G. Sharp. Westmoreland dismissed such critics and was firmly convinced that the Communists could be defeated by a war of attrition. Westmoreland's deputy and eventual replacement, General Creighton Abrams, dropped attrition as a strategy and instead focused the war effort on protecting the South Vietnamese people. One of the seriously under-reported stories of the war is how Abrams did this and brought America victory on the battlefield with ever smaller numbers of troops. Abrams deserves credit, but we also need to give Westmoreland his due. It is very possible that General Abrams' strategy might not have been quite so successful had Westmoreland not destroyed tens of thousands of Viet Cong soldiers (indeed, virtually eliminated the Viet Cong) and dozens of battalions of North Vietnamese regulars during his command. Westmoreland's attrition strategy, if carried to its logical conclusion—finding and destroying the enemy wherever they could be found, including sanctuaries and the North Vietnamese homeland—might have worked, had it not been politicized into a meaningless concept by the rules of "limited war."

Bound for Failure

Over two millennia ago, Sun Tzu prophetically described Westmoreland's plight. The Chinese sage wrote: "To put a rein on an able general while at the same time asking him to suppress a cunning enemy is like tying up the Black Hound of Han and then ordering him to catch elusive hares."[6]

China Beach Blanket Bingo

In March 1965, U.S. Marines landed at China Beach, Danang, South Vietnam. The landing was notable for the lack of any opposition—in fact, the

Marines were greeted by ubiquitous vendors of cheap food and souvenirs, pretty Vietnamese girls with flowers, and salty Army advisors gathered to shout disparaging remarks at the gear-laden young Marines. Ordered by President Johnson at the strong recommendation of the military, this marked the beginning of the U.S. commitment to "win" the Vietnam War for the South Vietnamese government. Ostensibly, the Marines were landing to provide protection for the vast airbase at Danang, increasingly used for missions into North Vietnam. Johnson still would not commit his troops to an unequivocal mission to defeat the Communists.

Their departure from the United States and their landing in Vietnam was not widely reported. Bui Diem, South Vietnam's ambassador to the United States, writes in his book *The Jaws of History* that South Vietnamese Prime Minister Phan Huy Quat learned of the Marines' landing on television.[7] In the United States, attention was drawn to the riots in Watts in California, and astronauts Gordon Cooper and Charles Conrad going into orbit in the Gemini 5 spacecraft. The film *The Sandpiper,* starring Richard Burton and Elizabeth Taylor, was showing in movie theaters. The Beatles were singing for *Help.* The Twins and the Dodgers were working their way to meeting in the World Series, and the Dow Jones Industrial Average had just broken 900.[8] Few Americans had ever heard, let alone spoken, the words "Viet Nam."

Unopposed the landing might have been, but it was only four months later that the Marines were severely tested in the first major battle for U.S. troops in Vietnam. It was Operation Starlite on the Van Tuong peninsula, fifty miles south of where they first landed, and nine miles south of Chu Lai, the Marine airbase.

On August 18, 1965, the Marines launched Operation Starlite, the first combined air and amphibious assault, and first regimental-sized operation, of the Vietnam War. The objective of the operation was to find and destroy the 1st Viet Cong Regiment, which, according to a Viet Cong deserter, was dug in on the Van Tuong peninsula, a position that could pose a potentially grave danger to the Marines at Chu Lai. The operation was a classic assault, with an amphibious landing on Green Beach, and simultaneous helicopter-borne landings one mile inland from the beach in three landing zones (LZs), Red, White, and Blue. A company of Marines formed a blocking force between the peninsula and Chu Lai, while the Marines dropped inland drove the Viet Cong to the coast and the waiting Marines at Green Beach. Naval gunfire from three ships offshore, air support from the Navy, Air Force, and Marine Corps, and artillery from the Marines supported the operation. The major combat took place on the first day of the assault, which saw a number of Marine units suffer up to 50 percent casualties. The primary helicopter unit, HMM 361 under the command of Lieutenant Colonel Lloyd

Starlite, Star Bright, First Order I Misread Tonight

The operations officer of the 3rd Marine Division picked the name "Satellite" for a military operation planned for August 1965. NASA was about to launch a Gemini spacecraft, and the operation itself consisted of two battalions from different regiments who would be "satellites" of the 7th Marine Headquarters. A failed generator caused the clerks to work by candlelight. Typing the official orders in the shadowy bunker, they misread *Satellite*, and the operation became *Starlite*.[9]

Childers, lifted the Marines into the three zones and flew resupply and medevac missions continuously. Fourteen of the eighteen helicopters from 361 were hit, with five pilots wounded and one crew member killed. By the end of the battle, fifty-two Marines were killed and more than 200 wounded. The Viet Cong left 600 dead on the battlefield. For their actions in the one day battle, two Marines received the Medal of Honor; six Navy Crosses were awarded, along with fourteen Silver Stars. The Marines who had come ashore to be greeted by flowers and young Vietnamese women only four months before now knew that Vietnam was not going to be a piece of cake. [I (the author) was there, a part of Starlite, and it was a revelation. Anyone who claimed that we were fighting a bunch of guys in their pajamas had no idea what they were talking about. These were hardened, disciplined, fanatically committed, well-armed, well-trained, well-supplied guerrillas who had been at war for decades—and learned something from the experience. They learned something else in this operation—though they could hit us hard, we could obliterate them in open combat.]

Just over two months after Starlite, the U.S. Army took on a North Vietnamese division in the Central Highlands of South Vietnam in what has often, mistakenly, been called the first major battle of the war. (It was the first major battle against the North Vietnamese Army. The enemy forces in Starlite were Viet Cong.) Large numbers of North Vietnamese troops were gathering in the central highlands with the idea of trying to cut South Vietnam in half. After failing in that mission—an attack on the Special Forces camp at Plei Me by the 32nd and 33rd NVA regiments was driven back—more than 1,700 North Vietnamese troops were withdrawing toward Cambodia. United States commanders saw a great opportunity to send elements of the First Cavalry Division to locate and engage the enemy. It would be a test of the Cavalry's new air mobile units. The battle took place in the Ia Drang valley, west of Pleiku.

Lieutenant Colonel Hal Moore led his 1st Battalion Seventh Cavalry (1/7) in an airmobile assault into the Ia Drang valley on the morning of November 14, 1965. The ensuing battle—centered in LZ X-Ray, where transport helicopters dropped Moore's troops—later became one of the most well-known of the war after a book by Moore and journalist Joe Galloway, *We Were Soldiers Once—And Young*, became a best-seller and was made into a feature film. Engaged in a bloody battle against a numerically superior enemy, the U.S. troops relied on overwhelming supporting firepower in the form of two batteries (twelve guns) of artillery from the 1st Battalion, 21st Artillery six miles away, and helicopter and fixed wing (Air Force) aerial artillery (rockets and bombs, including napalm), which was on call twenty-four hours a day.

Both sides claimed to have won the confrontation, which played out over four days. The Americans felt confident in their ability to engage superior (in number) Communist forces rapidly and efficiently, using their new air mobile cavalry supported by massive fire power; the Communists believed they had proved they could stand up to the vastly superior firepower of the Americans. The 7th Cavalry Regiment suffered a

Destroying Villages vs. Saving Them

After receiving an after action de-briefing from the Marine Corps on Operation Starlite, reporter Peter Arnett filed a story claiming the Marines had lost the battle, failed to rescue their wounded, and showed poor combat leadership.[10] The Marine Corps challenged Arnett's story; Arnett claimed he had "documentary proof" of its accuracy and offered to meet a Marine Corps press representative to produce it. A date was set, and Arnett didn't show up.

Arnett, who visited Hanoi in 1972 with American peace activists, was the reporter who claimed an American major had said (in 1968), "We had to destroy the village in order to save it." It now appears Arnett might have invented the quote to suit his own purposes.[11] One certainty is that the United States military saved more villages from the Communists than Arnett did.

Arnett won a Pulitzer Prize for International Reporting for his work in Vietnam. He finally got his (likely deserved) comeuppance in 1998 for narrating a program produced by CNN, *Time*, and *NewsStand*, which claimed that America had used lethal Sarin gas against a group of deserting U.S. soldiers in Laos in 1970. Arnett and several of the show's producers were fired by CNN, which retracted the contrived war crimes story.

higher percentage of casualties than had any regiment, Union or Confederate, at Gettysburg. During the Ia Drang campaign, which involved several such battles, the Communists lost more than 1,500 troops (normal combat ratios of the war would estimate their wounded at double that number). The Americans lost just over 300 killed in the campaign and more than 500 wounded. If the American strategy of search and destroy had weaknesses, one of them was *not* the skill and valor of American officers and soldiers.[12] The two North Vietnamese regiments that had tangled with the 7th Cavalry had been destroyed.

Though the North Vietnamese claimed to have won at Ia Drang (they claimed to win every battle they fought: Communist Propaganda 101), they immediately changed their military strategy. They gave up any hope of dividing South Vietnam or occupying any major part of it, because they didn't want to become targets for the Americans. In fact, not until their assault on Khe Sanh (where they lost 10,000 to 15,000 soldiers) almost three years later (January 21 to April 8, 1968) did they risk massing their troops against American forces.

Earlier heroics

Certainly the battles in Starlite and the Ia Drang Valley weren't the first serious attacks by the Communists. In spring 1964, Hanoi ordered the Viet Cong to increase the size and frequency of their attacks against the ARVN and their American advisors. The spring offensives proved to American observers, if any proof was needed, not only the seriousness of the Communist threat, but the South Vietnamese military's need for significant American assistance.

In July 1964, an attack on the Nam Dong Special Forces camp in Thua Thien province provided ample evidence of the value of American firepower and advisory support to the ARVN. Led by Captain Roger Donlon, the U.S. Special Forces detachment had two officers and ten NCOs advising a 300-man South Vietnamese Strike Force, with sixty Nung (Chinese mercenary) guards. Eight hundred Viet Cong breached portions of the camp and overran the Strike Force section of the camp, killing or wounding 100 members of the force and forcing the others to flee. But the section of the camp held by the Americans, with less than a tenth of the strength of the Communist attackers, refused to let the Viet Cong penetrate their perimeter. Sergeant Terrance Terrin, a medic, lost the use of an arm early in the battle but managed to fire his M-16 from the hip as the VC came across the fence, winning one of the five Silver Stars awarded for the battle.

Captain Donlon, braving what witnesses called the "extreme danger of intense Viet Cong fire from small arms, automatic weapons, and mortars," directed the defense of the Special Forces section of the camp. Although wounded four times, Captain Donlon threw back VC hand grenades, dragged a wounded sergeant, a 60mm mortar, a 57mm recoilless rifle, and boxes of ammunition to the rear, and rallied his men to a successful defense of their position. When daylight came, the Americans and Nungs directed massive air strikes against the exposed Viet Cong, driving them from the field. For his courage in this action, Captain Donlon became the first recipient of the Medal of Honor (the nation's highest award for valor in combat) awarded in the Vietnam War.

In July 1964, the Viet Cong launched more large attacks than it had launched in any previous month. Twelve of the attacks were of battalion strength (one thousand men) and seven were of company strength (two hundred men).[13] The acceleration and growing strength of Communist attacks, and the vast superiority of American discipline, fighting skills, and firepower over our ARVN allies—which

Books the Viet Cong Wouldn't Want You to Read

Jane Fonda's War, Mary Hershberger (The New Press, 2005). Even the North Vietnamese are embarrassed she supported them.

showed how American forces could tip the balance—weighed heavily on deliberations in Washington about our role in the conflict.

Hey, hey, LBJ, how in the heck did you get us into this mess?

If blame needs to be assigned for American involvement in the war (or better, the way we conducted it), there's plenty to go around: from the timid and uncertain responses of the Kennedy administration, to the internecine warfare between the State Department and the Pentagon, to the Kennedy administration's reluctant consent to overthrowing Diem. But what really set the course for the military floundering from 1965 to 1968 were the vagaries of the Johnson administration with its enormous domestic policy ambitions and its reliance on inexperienced egg-heads.

Vast theories aside, the dilemma the U.S. found itself in for the remainder of the Vietnam War was simple. The military (beginning with Westmoreland, Sharp, and the Joint Chiefs of Staff) viewed the war as a war like all others, with variations on weapons, topography, and resources—but the object was to defeat the enemy on the battlefield. The president and his advisors (McNamara, Rusk, and other civilians) saw the war as a tool that could be used to obtain a bargaining position in negotiations. For the military, the preferred strategy was to use massively superior power against the enemy and defeat him. The Johnson administration, however, wanted a limited war that assumed a reasonable enemy; America would gradually escalate its use of force, but withdraw it at any hint of negotiations from our opponent—which assumed that the enemy had an integrity of intent. Neither the U.S. military nor the Johnson administration got what it wanted. Westmoreland was forced to acquiesce to the politicians' desire to "limit" the war, and the administration was trying to negotiate with an enemy who never had any intention of negotiating an end to the war.

In 1964 the Vietnam War was Lyndon Johnson's War. Whatever mistakes, misjudgments, or errors Kennedy might have made, Johnson inherited a small, low intensity (from the U.S. viewpoint) battle from which he could reasonably have exited. He had, after all, run his 1964 presidential campaign against Barry Goldwater as the peace and domestic prosperity candidate, casting Goldwater as a war-mongering ultra-conservative who might stumble us into a nuclear catastrophe. But after the election, Johnson became more bellicose in his Vietnam references and ended up escalating American involvement to more than half a million troops on the ground in Southeast Asia; and he did this after repeated pledges that while he intended to help the South Vietnamese, he would not send "American boys" to do the job of "Asian boys." In his first address to Congress as president (November 27, 1963), he pledged: "This nation will keep its commitments from South Vietnam to West Berlin. We will be unceasing in the search for peace; resourceful in our pursuit of areas of agreement, even with those with whom we differ; and generous and loyal to those who join with us in common cause."

Certainly LBJ was aware of the growing problem in Vietnam. Early in his first year as president, in March 1964, his Secretary of Defense, Robert McNamara, returned from a trip to Vietnam with General Maxwell Taylor, the Chairman of the Joint Chiefs of Staff, and sent a memo to him stating bluntly:

"1. In terms of government control of the countryside, about 40 percent of the territory is under Viet Cong control... 2. Large groups of the population are now showing signs of apathy. 3. In the last ninety days, the weakening of the government's position has been particularly noticeable."[14] The

Books the Viet Cong Wouldn't Want You to Read

Our Vietnam Nightmare, Marguerite Higgins (Harper & Row, 1965).

Hint: The "nightmare" has to do with the U.S. State Department and the U.S. press. Higgins was one of the best war-correspondents of her time. And she knew Vietnam intimately.

Show Me the Numbers

The media liked to mock military press briefings, calling them "follies." But we know now that the "follies" were more accurate than the pages of the *New York Times* and the *Washington Post*. One of the most frequently mocked aspects of the military press conferences was alleged overstatements of how many enemy soldiers had been killed, the "body count." But from data assembled after the war, including from North Vietnamese sources, it seems as if the body count given by the U.S. military was *understated*.[26]

memo reiterated the dangers of Communist expansion and recommended using American force to curb it—though, again, this force was to be calibrated rather than massive. The day following his receipt of the memo, Johnson approved it as National Security Action Memorandum (NSAM) 288.

Later (when published in 1971), the Pentagon Papers (a collection of 7,000 pages of U.S. military, administration and state department memos and analyses which McNamara had ordered assembled and which documented the history of the U.S. commitment in Vietnam. Later stolen and given to the *New York Times*) described NSAM 288: "In enunciating the policies of NSAM-288 we had rhetorically committed ourselves to do whatever was needed to achieve our stated objectives in South Vietnam. The program decided upon and spelled out in NSAM-288 reflected our recognition that the problem was greater than we had previously supposed, and that the progress that we had previously thought we were making was more apparent than real. The program constituted a larger effort than we had undertaken before; it corresponded to our increased estimates of the magnitude of the task before us. Nevertheless, we might have chosen to do more along the lines of what we did decide to do, and above all we might have chosen to do some things that we specifically chose not to do at this time (although we began to plan for some of these on a contingency basis). If there were to be new or greater problems in the future it was because we did not correctly appraise the magnitude of the problem nor fully foresee the complexity of the difficulties we faced. There were indeed some who believed that the program we decided upon was not enough, notably the JCS who had gone on record that until aid to the VC from outside of South Vietnam was cut off, it would be impossible to eliminate the insurgency there. But the program as decided upon in 288 did correspond to the official consensus that this was a prescription suited to the illness as we diagnosed it."[15]

Any argument that Johnson was misled or misinformed about the situation he had inherited in South Vietnam would seem to be unfounded. But distracted by his passionate (and ultimately successful) drive to pass the Civil Rights Act of 1964, Johnson's contribution to the war effort consisted of agreeing to a gradual implementation of force against the Viet Cong and the North Vietnamese. As one of the most successful and powerful members of Congress in the history of the United States, Johnson believed that his powers of persuasion and expertise in pushing his agenda through with reluctant fellow politicians would work equally well with the Communist leaders in Hanoi, especially since the forces at his disposal were not mere bullying, arm-twisting, or denying special political projects, but military power. If he could work his will on Congress, he could surely work it on the "tin horn leader"[16] of some "pissant"[17] Asian country. But Congress played by the rules. Hanoi didn't have the same respect for parliamentary procedure, or elections, or the big-eared leader of some giant American country.

Instead, the Communists were relentlessly focused on their objective of conquering South Vietnam, and to that end, they increased their raids and attacks throughout the country. On February 3, 1964, they attacked the American compound at Kontum City; on February 7, the Viet Cong exploded a bomb in a Saigon theater patronized exclusively by Americans; in April the area around Saigon became so dangerous that a special zone of defense was set up; a week later the Viet Cong captured Kien Long and killed 300 South Vietnamese soldiers; on May 2, a Viet Cong underwater demolition team sank (temporarily) the USS *Card*, while she was berthed in Saigon; and on July 4, a Viet Cong regiment overran the Special Forces Camp at Nam Dong, killing two of the American advisors.

It was obvious that rather than avoiding antagonizing the Americans in South Vietnam, the Communists were deliberately targeting them—in order to see what President Johnson's reaction might be. There was no American military reprisal after any of these events. It was a presidential election year and Johnson wanted no crisis over Vietnam. Polls showed that more than two-thirds of the American public paid no attention to Vietnam.[18] Johnson was content to let it remain that way. Critics and pundits later called the war a "war of lost opportunities" referring primarily to the Communists' occasional offers (fraudulent, as we would find out) of negotiations. A more likely lost opportunity was the opportunity to convince Hanoi in 1964 that any attacks on U.S. facilities and troops would lead to massive retaliation on North Vietnamese targets. Documents available to historians after the war revealed that Hanoi was vitally concerned about the depth of America's commitment to the defense of South Vietnam. Early in the war, we gave a lukewarm impression, an impression institutionalized by our acceptance of a "graduated escalation" strategy. A better strategy would have been massive retaliation, not only to protect American troops, but to prove to the Communist government in Hanoi that it would have to accept the existence of an independent South Vietnam—or face the obliteration of the North Vietnamese capital. When we at least feigned that sort of approach, with the Christmas bombing of 1972, under Nixon, we got results. Before that, the air war in Vietnam had different objectives.

Air War Vietnam

During the 1960s, the United States launched three major, sustained aerial bombardment campaigns against the enemy in North Vietnam and Laos. These campaigns and their effectiveness are shrouded in misconception and ignorance like so many of America's efforts in the war. The three, Operation Rolling Thunder, Operation Barrel Roll, and Operation Steel Tiger, were largely successful and undoubtedly effective, given the overall strategy (which few military men agreed with) of a limited war. The measure of success was what they prevented, not what they accomplished.

Primarily, the bombing campaigns were designed to intimidate the Communist leadership in Hanoi (in which they were not very effective) and to interdict the supply chain of troops and materiel flowing from North Vietnam into Laos, Cambodia, and South Vietnam. The effectiveness for the interdiction campaign should be measured by the fact that throughout the war the Communists were never able to assemble a fighting unit large enough and with enough logistical support to mount a threat to the American and Allied forces within South Vietnam. Tens of thousands of enemy combatants and millions of tons of food and war materiel were destroyed en route to the South.

The destruction of North Vietnam, in the same way Allied bombing leveled large swathes of Germany and Japan in World War II, was never

Close Air Support

The close air support of Allied troops in South Vietnam by the Air Force, Army, Navy, and Marine Corps was the single most effective weapon in the war. Thousands upon thousands of soldiers and Marines in combat in South Vietnam owe their lives to the exceptional skill, daring, and persistence of American pilots and crewmen who were on call almost twenty-four hours a day, seven days a week, to provide assistance with rockets, bombs, guns, and medical evacuation.

permitted as an objective. No population centers were targeted. No scorched earth policies were ever seriously considered.

Much has been made of the total tonnage of bombs dropped by American forces during the war. But the majority of that tonnage (Laos received the most of it) was dropped on a jungle canopy in sparsely populated areas. So yes, more tonnage might have been dropped in the Vietnam War than in World War II, but the targeted areas were so vastly different as to make comparisons specious.

Rolling (intermittent with light showers) *Thunder,* March 1965 to November 1968

Early in the morning of February 7, 1965, the Viet Cong struck at the United States airfield at Pleiku, in the central highlands, and at the helicopter base at Camp Holloway, four miles away. Nine Americans were killed and seventy-six were wounded and evacuated. Sixteen helicopters and six fixed-wing aircraft were damaged or destroyed. After tolerating so many earlier attacks on Americans, President Johnson finally ordered a reprisal air strike (Operation *Flaming Dart*)—but it was a weak and ineffectual effort against low priority targets. On February 10, the Viet Cong attacked the enlisted men's billet at Qui Nhon, on the coast of South Vietnam, killing twenty-three American soldiers and wounding twenty-one others. In reply, the president authorized an attack on North Vietnamese army barracks (Operation *Flaming Dart II*).

Then, on February 13, 1965, President Johnson ordered a "program of measured and limited air action jointly with the GVN [the government of South Vietnam] against selected targets in the DRV [North Vietnam]." The program was called *Rolling Thunder* and it would last with (politically motivated) stoppages and starts for the next three-and-a-half years.[19]

In August 1964, the Joint Chiefs had created a wish list of ninety-four targets—bridges, supply dumps, railroads, shipping docks—that they

1, 2, 3, 4, What Are We Fighting For?

One of the great myths of the Vietnam War is that the North Vietnamese troops were great fighters because they knew exactly what they were fighting for, and our troops didn't. In fact, the North Vietnamese troops were largely uneducated, indoctrinated by the Communist state, and had no choice but to obey the dictates of the brutal totalitarian government that sent them South where hundreds of thousands of them died. American troops on the other hand, if you had asked them, could tell you why Communism was bad and why we had to stop its violent spread. American troops knew what they were fighting for—what they didn't understand was the LBJ/McNamara strategy, if it can be called that, of attrition; on-again, off-again bombing; and taking ground only to leave it.

wanted to destroy. It could be done, they said, in an eight-week campaign. Johnson and McNamara, however, fell prey to the bugaboo that had haunted America in the Korean War—what if Red China intervened, or Soviet Russia, or what if such strikes lit the fuse for World War III? In fact, none of these outcomes were likely. But *Rolling Thunder* was, essentially, the Johnson and McNamara version of what the Joint Chiefs wanted: a bombing campaign, but gradual, with each target to be cleared by the president and the secretary of defense down to the level of what sort of planes and bombs should be used and what time they would strike. Really important targets, like North Vietnamese airfields, or the capital, Hanoi, or North Vietnam's chief port, Haiphong, were not only off-limits but given a clear cordon or buffer zone, as was North Vietnam's border with China.

While our pilots bombed blindfolded or with one jet engine tied behind their backs, the risks they ran were enormous. The North Vietnamese had

Soviet-made MiG fighters, not to mention surface-to-air missiles and anti-aircraft batteries. Particularly when Rolling Thunder was expanded to hit targets farther north and to hit targets of real value, like MiG airfields in 1967 and 1968, our pilots were in a fully fledged high-risk air war over the skies of Vietnam. Because so much of the operation was stop and go, as Washington hoped for negotiations, our progress was necessarily limited, because the North Vietnamese were given time to rearm for the next ratcheting up of the bombing. If *Rolling Thunder* was a failure, it was only because it was designed in such a way by McNamara and Johnson that it had to fail—the pressure it was meant to apply to Hanoi was utterly insufficient and completely misread the enemy. Still, we should recognize that the incredible skill and courage of American pilots and crews and support personnel were what brought the United States to victory in 1973, before the politicians gave it all away again.

Operation *Barrel Roll*, December 1964 to March 1973

Barrel Roll was a covert U.S. Air Force and Navy aerial operation implemented in northeastern Laos in 1964 to interdict supplies and troops moving out of North Vietnam, down the Ho Chi Minh Trail, and into South Vietnam. *Barrel Roll* pilots also ended up providing close air support for the Royal Lao Army and anti-Communist Laotian tribes fighting the Pathet Lao and the North Vietnamese. The operation was a closely held secret because of the alleged neutrality of Laos. The manifest reality on the ground, however, was that the North Vietnamese not only had 40,000 troops fighting alongside the Communist Pathet Lao to overthrow the Laotian government, but were using Laos as a supply line and staging area for their ongoing invasion of South Vietnam.

For a covert operation, it wasn't very secretive. Any visitor to Vientianne, the administrative capital of Laos, would find scores of American airmen in the bars and restaurants of that city, and dozens of military-type aircraft landing and taking off from the airport. *Time* magazine even ran an article in 1968 detailing the air war in Laos.

The North Vietnamese tried to keep their own involvement secret as well, but they were even less covert than we were. Hanoi wanted to maintain the fiction that it respected Laotian neutrality—both in order to maintain a modicum of international respectability and to allow it to insist that the conflict in South Vietnam was a popular uprising, not a Northern invasion. That was completely and utterly false, but trying to maintain that falsehood encouraged Hanoi to treat its involvement in Laos as a limited war. The NVA could have conquered Laos at any point; but for North Vietnam the priority was to maintain the Ho Chi Minh Trail. Toppling the Laotian domino could come later.

In our case, we operated with the support of the Laotian government. The Laotian Prime Minister Souvanna Phouma gave operation *Barrel Roll* the thumbs up on December 12, 1964. *Barrel Roll* was conducted with a minimum of bureaucracy and a certain panache—almost as if the Flying Tigers had been reincarnated (and given helicopters) to fight in Laos. This was largely a CIA and Air Force operation, supported not only by the Laotian government, but by the Thai government, which, being near the firing line, had a much greater belief in the domino theory than liberal professors stateside. In this crazy little corner of the war you could have witnessed aerial combat between Americans (who supposedly weren't there) and North Vietnamese

The Rescue of Streetcar 304

Navy pilot Lieutenant Kenny Fields, flying an A-7, was shot down at Techpone, Laos, in May 1968, on his first combat mission off the carrier USS *America*. Shortly thereafter a rescue pilot was shot down nearby. By the time Fields' rescue was complete (forty hours after he ejected) the Air Force had flown 189 sorties, four pilots had been shot down, and seven aircraft were lost or heavily damaged in the effort to rescue him. One of the pilots shot down became a POW for five years.

(who equally supposedly weren't there), the latter using Soviet-built planes and equipment in "neutral" Laos.

For as long as we were engaged in Vietnam, *Barrel Roll* kept the Communists from toppling the Laotian government, and in the process, provided a shield to Thailand. It was also an effective check on the Ho Chi Minh Trail.

Operation *Steel Tiger*, April 1965 to November 1968

As the operational responsibilities in *Barrel Roll* increased rapidly, the 7th Air Force and U.S. Navy Task Force 77 launched Operation *Steel Tiger* in the southeastern portion of Laos. The sole purpose of *Steel Tiger* was to find and destroy enemy traffic on the Ho Chi Minh Trail. Although the mission was not complicated by any close air support operations, *Steel Tiger*'s Tactical Area of Responsibility (TAOR) contained the most lethal concentration of Communist anti-aircraft defenses outside of the Hanoi area. Some of the most dramatic and gut-wrenching rescues of downed American pilots took place in this area. By the end of *Steel Tiger* (absorbed into Operation *Commando Hunt* in 1967) more than 130 U.S. aircraft and helicopters had been shot down in the operation (compare that to 131 lost aircraft in Operation *Barrel Roll*, which lasted nearly nine years).[20]

Tet

The situation in South Vietnam in 1967 was far from dire for the Americans and their allies. Although Westmorland's war of attrition was not spectacular and the bombing in the North produced no immediately dramatic results, the Viet Cong were being ground out of existence. The majority of the South Vietnamese countryside was under the uneasy control of the South Vietnamese government. None of the major cities in the

South felt threatened by an imminent attack of significant size. Hanoi was well aware that it had not prevailed in any major engagement against the United States.

But the North Vietnamese also noticed the development of an anti-war movement in the United States, and they quickly latched onto this as the lever to separate America from South Vietnam. They decided to jump on one end of that lever by launching a massive surprise attack during the Vietnamese holiday of Tet, a period when Communist and South Vietnam forces agreed to a cease-fire (which the Communists obviously had no intention of keeping) and South Vietnamese troops went on leave in large numbers. It became the turning point of the war—not because of what happened on the battlefield, but because of how the media utterly missed the real story of Tet and reported its own sense of panic and doom, which didn't accord with the facts on the ground.

On January 30, 1968, the Viet Cong hit Danang and Hoi An in I Corps (northern South Vietnam) and cities in II Corps down the coast. The next

What Happened to the Viet Cong?

When the People's Army of Vietnam published its official history of the war, it never used the terms Viet Cong, South Vietnamese Liberation Army, or North Vietnamese Army. Instead it treated all Communist military forces as components of itself. The idea that the Viet Cong were a self-sustaining, independent, "people's movement," is a fiction that not even the Communist Vietnamese government bothers to maintain. It can be found now only among aging radicals in political science departments on college campuses.

night, they continued the attacks, hitting more than 100 cities throughout Vietnam including Hue, Ben Tre, and Saigon, where targets included the U.S. Embassy and the Presidential Palace. All hell seemed to have broken loose.

The Tet Offensive gave the press corps the war they had been waiting to cover: burning buildings, destroyed neighborhoods, to-the-death fire fights, tracers overhead, thumps of artillery, dead and wounded bodies of VC, civilians, and U.S. soldiers on the streets of Saigon and Hue. It made for dramatic pictures, dramatic stories, and dramatic television, all played out not in some inaccessible jungle or rice paddy, but right in front of them.

The battle at the U.S. Embassy, which the correspondents knew well, took center stage. The embassy compound, half a dozen buildings surrounded by an eight foot fence, was in the heart of Saigon, not far from the news bureaus. Just after midnight on January 30, a nineteen-man Viet Cong sapper team attacked the embassy. The enemy sappers were able to breach the wall and break into the compound. MPs and Marine reinforcements arrived and fought a gun battle with the VC, the last of whom was found dead about six hours later. Belatedly, at 11:45 a.m., the American flag was raised in front of the embassy, to show the city that the embassy compound had been secured.

Chateau de Carnage

Laments about the destruction of South Vietnamese villages, neighborhoods, and countryside were a constant in reporting about the war. Few reporters, apparently, had ever seen photographs of the rubble of liberated Europe in the Second World War. War means fighting, and fighting means killing, as a famous Confederate cavalry officer, Nathan Bedford Forrest, once said.[22] And that means buildings, houses, and trees get destroyed, too. Southerners—in America, not Vietnam—might remember that Atlanta, and a heap of countryside and Southern towns got put to the torch in the wake of General Sherman's march to the sea. But liberal reporters seemed to share the Johnson administration's misplaced hope that war could be carefully controlled, limited, and really amount to little more than a polite argument conducted with bombs pinpointed to explode in isolated areas.

The sappers had never actually made it into the embassy building, though early headlines said they had, and some reporters even ran with stories about gun battles up and down the embassy's carpeted halls. The message of the reporting was clear, if inaccurate—how can the United States win the war if it can't even defend its own embassy?

Early news reports had Saigon as a city in flames. The Cholon district of Saigon was in sad shape to be sure. But an estimated 90 percent of Saigon was relatively untouched. The Viet Cong, sometimes in civilian clothes, certainly created havoc, running around the city, targeting ARVN and South Vietnamese police for execution. For the press, however, the most infamous executioner was General Nguyen Ngoc Loan, a Saigon policeman who shot a Viet Cong "suspect" on a Saigon street. The Viet Cong had reportedly just shot an ARVN lieutenant and his family. General Loan was well within his rights of summarily executing an enemy soldier caught in civilian clothing, but the Pulitzer Prize-winning photo capturing the incident became part of the Left's indictment of the war (even though the photographer himself thought Loan was a hero and apologized to him for the way the photo had been used to ruin the general's reputation).[21]

The other focal point for reporters was the extended battle at Hue, the old imperial capital in northern South Vietnam. The Viet Cong captured the city during the Tet offensive and were not driven out for almost a month, and then only after the bloodiest battle American troops had yet fought in Vietnam. U.S. Marines finally recaptured the city by going house to house after massive shelling (mostly by ARVN artillery) against its Communist-occupied neighborhoods. The American media came to the amazing discovery that war can cause damage to property—though they often blamed that destruction on the city's liberators rather than its attackers. In fact, throughout the Vietnam War, the American media emphasized the destruction of the Vietnam countryside and villages, barely mentioning the invasion and occupation by the North Vietnamese, which brought the U.S. military into the picture to begin with.

The tragedy of Hue, its big story, largely ignored by the media, was not the loss of buildings; it was the discovery of thousands of its citizens buried in mass graves—the victims of the VC and NVA who had simply murdered those they considered class enemies of the Communists in South Vietnam: government officials, teachers, urban professionals, policemen, and others. It took a British journalist, Stewart Harris (who opposed American policy in Vietnam and said, "My instinct is not to sustain it by writing propaganda"[23]) to launch an investigation into the Communist atrocities and report on them. According to Peter Braestrup, the foremost authority on media coverage of the Tet Offensive, it was apparently the only investigation undertaken at the time. To its credit, *Time* magazine picked up Stewart Harris's story from the *Times* of London.

The North Vietnamese Army and the Vietcong executed many Vietnamese, some Americans, and a few other foreigners during the fighting in and around Hue. I am sure of this after spending several days in Hue investigating allegations of killings and torture. I saw and photographed a lot for myself, but inevitably I relied on many civilians and soldiers, Vietnamese, Americans, Australians, and others. All seemed honest witnesses, telling the truth as they believed it.... Summing up all this evidence about the behavior of the Vietcong and the North Vietnamese Army in Hue, one thing is abundantly clear and ought to surprise no one. They put into practice, with their usual efficiency, the traditional communist policy of punishing by execution selected leaders who support their enemies. In Hue, as elsewhere, they were unable on the whole to capture and execute the more important officials, because these men were careful to protect themselves in heavily fortified compounds, defended by soldiers and police. In Hue, as elsewhere, the more defenseless "little people" were the victims—the village and hamlet chiefs, the teachers, and the policemen.[24]

Not only did most of the media ignore the massacre at Hue, they also utterly ignored one of its logical implications: that perhaps America's involvement in defending South Vietnam was a noble cause after all; maybe we were fighting against a cruel and vicious enemy that was in the service of an aggressive, hateful ideology with designs on enslaving other peoples and other countries; maybe—just maybe—we were doing the right thing.

And there was an even bigger story the media missed; and this one was more consequential. In Saigon, within two weeks of the initial fighting, it became apparent that the giant Communist surprise attack had been a disaster for the Viet Cong, whose losses were catastrophic. The VC held Hue for nearly a month, but at the cost of near annihilation. In South Vietnam's other cities, and in the countryside, the VC were swiftly defeated. From a military point of view, the Tet Offensive was a massive Communist defeat, both in terms of casualties and in proving that if the people of South Vietnam were ever to rise up, it would be against the Communists, not for them. But General Giap (the supreme North Vietnamese military commander for much of the war) was playing for other stakes. He might have been crushed on the battlefield, but he believed the center of the war was not in Saigon, but in America and its public opinion. His goals in the Tet Offensive, as he stated on many occasions, were to spark an uprising against the South Vietnamese government (that didn't work), to

Hope They Showed Its Good Side

In the reporting of the battle at Khe Sanh, the smoldering carcass of the *only* C-130 shot down in the long siege was used as the background for dozens of reports for television audiences over the next few weeks, subtly implying that C-130s were being shot down with horrifying regularity.

demoralize the ARVN (that didn't work either, as the ARVN performed more than credibly in Tet, when their own homes and families were on the line), and to weaken the will of the American people to carry on the war. On this last point, he succeeded. The American media convinced the American public that the 1968 Tet Offensive was a disaster for America and its South Vietnamese allies.

Contrary to misguided public opinion at the time, the American generals were not taken by surprise. General Earle Wheeler, chairman of the Joint Chiefs of Staff, and General William Westmoreland had spoken publicly and privately in the months before Tet about the distinct possibility of a major push by the NVA. The media all but ignored them. President Johnson confided to Australian officials that he expected attacks in Vietnam. That was one reason why the American response during Tet was so effective.

But the newsmen reported what was in front of them, which appeared to be chaos and catastrophe. Most of them had never seen combat up close before. They never stepped back to look at the big picture. They discounted reports from the military as "cover-your-ass" propaganda. As reporters will, they leapt at stories of disaster as making good copy.

To be fair, in terms of human suffering, there was plenty of good copy to be had. Aside from the devastating loss of homes, businesses, and personal property, the number of South Vietnamese civilians killed and wounded during Tet amounted to tens of thousands. The American press accurately portrayed the pathos and suffering of the South Vietnamese people. The South Vietnamese military suffered 2,788 killed and more than 8,000 wounded. America and other Allied forces suffered 1,536 killed and more than 7,500 wounded. After years of hearing that progress was being made in South Vietnam, the American people were shown a picture of destruction and chaos, of rubble and refugees, of gunfights in the streets. What they didn't learn, until much later, was that the Communists' brutal attack spelled virtually the end of the Viet Cong as a viable fighting force. From a military point of view, the Communist attack was an exercise in futility. The Communists had spent six months of humping 81,000 tons of supplies down the Ho Chi Minh Trail to support the Tet Offensive; 150,000 Viet Cong and another 150,000 North Vietnamese had been thrown into the attack; and what they achieved were losses of 75,000 to 80,000 men. When all was said and done, they had not held onto a single South Vietnamese city. Wasn't that the story of Tet?

Evidently not, according to the majority of the opinion makers, led by Walter Cronkite of CBS News, "the most trusted man in America." Returning from a brief trip to Vietnam, Cronkite voiced his "gloomy conclusions" on a special report aired February 27, 1968: "It is increasingly clear... that the only rational way out...will be to negotiate, not as victors, but as an honorable people who lived up to their pledge to defend democracy, and did the best they could."[25]

"Hanoi, Answer Your Damn Phone!"

During the Johnson administration alone, there were sixteen bombing halts (to give Hanoi a reason to negotiate) and seventy-two peace initiatives. Johnson in his memoirs said, "Never once was there a clear sign that Ho Chi Minh had a genuine interest in bargaining for peace."[27]

In other words, sure we had just beaten the VC/NVA to a bloody pulp, but defending democracy was proving to be just too damn hard.

If, as some claim, the Cronkite broadcast was the point where public opinion tipped against the war, one wonders what would have happened if he had accurately reported the situation:

> I have returned from a trip to South Vietnam to see the results of the brutal Communist attack on that country. The Tet Offensive clearly indicates that the North Vietnamese are dedicated to taking over the sovereign nation of South Vietnam (so recognized by the United Nations). But I can report honestly that

the Communist aggressors, in what was obviously a desperate action, hold no cities in the South (with the exception of Hue where there are reports of mass executions of civilians) and were soundly defeated on the battlefield. The ARVN units fought bravely and well with the support of our American forces. There were few, if any, defections of South Vietnamese, military or civilian, to the side of the Communists as they have been preaching there would certainly be. Clearly the South Vietnamese people do not desire to live under a Communist dictatorship.

One would hope that the United States will take advantage of this devastating blow to the enemies of South Vietnam, clean out the Communists' sanctuaries, close the Communists' supply chains, and bring an end to the Communists' bloody, illegal, inhuman, and indecent attacks. South Vietnam is a friendly nation that has sought and needs our assistance. This is the action President Kennedy pledged to the world, and it is our duty to honor that pledge.

And that's the way it really is.

But that's not what he said. Instead, Cronkite seemed to take what became the liberal view of the Vietnam War: it didn't matter that the South Vietnamese might be sacrificed to the Communists who would butcher them, send them to reeducation camps—where anti-Communist attitudes would be beaten out of them through political indoctrination sessions, punctuated by back-breaking work (sometimes to the point of death), and endless punishments and harassments—and incarcerate them in a totalitarian regime. No, what mattered was that we simply get out of the mess, because then we wouldn't be responsible for any of the killing or the destruction that went along with war, media men like Cronkite wouldn't need to cover it so closely, and draft boards wouldn't be pulling names of kids to be packed aboard cargo planes and sent to fight in southeast Asia. One can understand that point of view, but it does seem a trifle parochial, especially given John F. Kennedy's commitment to South Vietnam; and you can understand why our South Vietnamese allies might not have appreciated it. Let's give up, Cronkite said, in essence, and his

A Frank, Reasoned Discussion

After a careful and extensive study of the situation in Southeast Asia, the Joint Chiefs of Staff unanimously concluded that the risk of Chinese or Soviet "over-reaction" to America's efforts in Vietnam was minimal. It was decided, therefore, that the way to fight the war was massive aerial attacks on Hanoi and the mining and closure of the North Vietnamese ports of entry to slow or stop arms and supplies being shipped from other Communist countries to aid the North Vietnamese.

In November 1965, the Joint Chiefs requested and received permission to present their findings to President Lyndon Johnson in the White House. After listening inattentively for a short while, Johnson responded: "He screamed obscenities, he cursed them personally.... He called them filthy names— sh*theads, dumb sh*ts, pompous a**holes—and used 'the F-word' as an adjective more freely than a Marine in boot camp would use it.... He told them he was disgusted with their naïve approach, and that he was not going to let some military idiots talk him into World War III. He ended the conference by shouting 'Get the hell out of my office!'"

Eight years and 350,000 U.S. casualties (including almost 60,000 dead) later President Nixon ended the war in Vietnam using exactly the same tactics that Johnson so denigrated.[28]

status and persona meant that his message did more damage to the successful conclusion of the Vietnam War than did the antics of anti-war figures like Jane Fonda and Daniel Ellsberg.

Chapter Four

UNHERALDED VICTORY, 1968–1973

In the wake of the Tet Offensive, an intelligent observer—of which there seemed to be very few—might have asked: "What were the Communists thinking? What did they hope to achieve? Why did they think they could defeat the most powerful nation on earth—when they had lost every significant battle against U.S. troops since 1965?"

The answers to those questions would have been interesting and instructive. Instead, most reporters ran with their prejudices—and most reporters were liberal and opposed to the war. Liberal pundits were almost gleeful in trumpeting that they had been right all along—even though they hadn't been—in doubting General Westmoreland's optimism about our military progress. Indeed, one little-noticed irony was that Vietnam started as a liberals' war, was fought by General Westmoreland in a liberal way (with innumerable constraints on the use of force, civilian micromanaging, and the export of Great Society programs to South Vietnam). And yet liberals themselves led the charge to repudiate their own war and all the people who conducted it for them.

The reason why

One unpopular answer as to why North Vietnam launched the Tet Offensive was that the Communists had fallen prey to one of the failings of a

Guess what?

‡ President Lyndon Johnson did not run for a second term because of despair over a massive American victory (which he didn't recognize, because he got his news from television)

‡ President Richard Nixon won the Vietnam War while rapidly withdrawing American troops

‡ North Vietnamese general Vo Nguyen Giap conquered South Vietnam only because the U.S. Democratic Congress refused to live up to its treaty obligations

What in the Heck Were the Communists Thinking?

A U.S. Army intelligence officer, who had seen all of the evidence of the forthcoming Tet Offensive, was quoted as admitting, "If we'd gotten the whole battle plan, it wouldn't have been credible to us." That Hanoi should (after years of defeats on the battlefield) launch an all-out assault was as unthinkable as if a chess player, about to be checked in a championship tourney, should suddenly send board and pieces flying with a sweep of his hand and leap across the table to grab his opponent by the throat.[1]

dictatorship—they had come to believe their own propaganda, and also what they read in the Western press. Throughout the long war, the media focused on American mistakes—imagined or real—and rarely considered the idiocy of the Hanoi brain-trust. In retrospect, almost every one of General Giap's campaigns in the war were blunders of epic proportions resulting in horrific losses of men and material, (the *lowest* estimate shows ten enemy troops killed for every American soldier who was killed). It wasn't tactical or strategic brilliance that brought North Vietnam victory over South Vietnam.

In the South, General Nguyen Chi Thanh, leader of the Communist efforts, experienced first hand the overwhelming destruction which American technology (air power and artillery) could bring to bear on any battle, anywhere in the country. The helicopter-supported mobility of the American forces harried the Communists who always supposed they had the advantages of choosing where to fight and being able to retreat safely. But the American strategy of search-and-destroy methodically chewed his troops to pieces—and if he had not had the sanctuaries of Cambodia and Laos, Thanh knew the odds against him would have been even worse. His counsel, which he repeatedly sent to the Hanoi politburo, was not to form up for major battles, but to regress to the first stage of the Communist strategy—small unit tactics and lightning strikes.

Thanh's arguments did not win support because there was little to encourage Hanoi about the military or political situation in South Vietnam in 1968. Hanoi believed major engagements were needed to keep the war on the front pages of American newspapers and the 6:00 news.

South Vietnam wasn't cooperating. After Nguyen Van Thieu took power in South Vietnam as head of state in 1965 and president (through elections) in 1967, there were no more coups. There were also no mass uprisings against the government of South Vietnam despite the Communists' desire for the opportunities social unrest provided. In fact, the South Vietnamese people were beginning to believe they had a chance of a stable government. There was no reason for them to support the Viet Cong—except by compulsion, given the VC's assassinations, forced recruitments, and general cruelty—and there was certainly no reason, unless you were a committed Communist, to support the conquest of South Vietnam by the North Vietnamese.

Hanoi itself had experienced only highly restricted, and therefore largely ineffective, bombing raids in North Vietnam, which, though damaging, were not going to stop Hanoi's war efforts. Thanks to its unending supply of anti-aircraft weaponry, including surface to air missiles, radar, and bountiful ammunition, Hanoi felt somewhat insulated from the bloody cost of the war. The troops they lost in the South were treated as cannon fodder; there was no sentimentality in Hanoi.

This is not to say that military officials in Hanoi didn't realize they had severe problems. Most of them agreed with General Thanh's assessment of the futility of continued large scale combat against the Americans. The crossover point of losses to replacements (new soldiers for those lost)

I Only Believe What I Read in the Newspapers

Another irony is that the biased reporting of the major American media led Hanoi to actually believe that American forces were misled, weak and demoralized, ill-suited to jungle warfare, and could be beaten by the dedicated true-believers fed into battles by the Communist leaders. "Oops," as General Giap might have said, "I just lost another 10,000 men. Oh well, plenty more where they came from."

was becoming impossible to ignore. The losses in the South were approaching 200,000 a year, roughly matching the number of young men reaching the age of seventeen each year, the age of conscription. A logical, reasonable regime, such as Johnson and McNamara dreamed they were dealing with, would certainly have considered negotiating an end to the war and the horrific burden on its people. But the Communists were neither reasonable nor logical, which is why a strategy of attrition and graduated escalations to encourage negotiations was utterly misbegotten. The Communists were fanatic believers in the justness of their cause and the inevitability of their triumph—and the anti-war movement in the West encouraged their sense of inevitable victory.

So it was a combination of hubris and ego, the advanced age of the leaders (who desperately wanted to experience the thrill of defeating the United States) wanting to achieve (at a minimum) a huge public relations victory in the West (the one victory they did win), and, from a purely military point of view, horrible miscalculation that led them to launch an all-out offensive against South Vietnam.

Vo Nguyen Giap, the most respected military leader in Hanoi, was chosen to plan and lead the offensive. Giap's strategy was the same he had used against the French: stage a diversion to draw troops away from the highly populated areas and then attack those areas. His diversion during Tet was to draw the Americans to Khe Sanh, where the U.S. Marines had fortified an area just below the DMZ astride a major South Vietnamese highway leading from the Vietnam coast into a growing Communist supply depot at Tchepone, Laos. Giap's nostalgic plan actually worked—up to a point. The United States military and the Johnson administration believed that a major assault would take place against the Marines. Their fear of another "Dien Bien Phu" even caused President Johnson to take the highly unusual (in the U.S. military) position of having American commanders guarantee in writing that they could successfully defend Khe Sanh.

Giap had a problem—that problem was reality. The United States had thousands of well-trained and well-armed Marines at Khe Sanh. They had unlimited air power, including B-52s. They had enormous naval gunfire available from offshore. And they had a huge reserve of troops that could be moved rapidly by helicopter into the Khe Sanh battle.

A Communist Kind of Caring

William Bundy observed that in the Tet Offensive "the North Vietnamese fought to the last Viet Cong."[2]

The Giap strategy did have elements that could lead to success. He believed the Johnson administration would not commit more troops to South Vietnam. If Giap could create the illusion that America's position in South Vietnam was untenable short of an immediate infusion of troops, the Johnson administration would be forced to confess that America's commitment to South Vietnam was limited and ending. Giap was also convinced that the Johnson administration would not endanger North Vietnam's sanctuaries across the DMZ or in Cambodia or (in any serious way) in Laos. Finally, he believed that growing anti-war sentiment in the United States and the political pressures on Johnson in an election year, particularly on his left flank, could force the administration to withdraw from South Vietnam in the wake of a large-scale Communist victory. The irony, of course, is that the Tet Offensive was a large-scale Communist defeat—yet it still eviscerated the morale of the Johnson administration and convinced Johnson not to run for reelection. Had the United States followed up the destruction of the Viet Cong in the Tet Offensive by mining Haiphong Harbor and bombing Hanoi (as Nixon did in 1972), the war might have ended in 1968.

But that didn't happen. Instead, the Communists, with their lack of tactical options—short of, from a strategic perspective, human wave attacks—began another series of offensive actions in May 1968, striking mostly around Saigon. In the first two weeks of this new offensive, they lost more than 12,000 men. Former NVA Colonel Bui Tin, writing after the war, said, "Nor did we learn from the military failures of the Tet Offensive. Instead, although we had lost the element of surprise, we went on to mount further major attacks in May and September 1968 and suffered even heavier losses."[3]

When Westmoreland left Vietnam, having been "kicked upstairs" in being promoted to Army Chief of Staff, many in the Johnson administration considered him a failure. But Westmoreland left behind him a defeated enemy; it was his political masters who failed. Westmoreland did his job. President Johnson and his administration did not do theirs—and perhaps could not do theirs because they had no realistic strategic vision and an underlying weakness of commitment when it came to "pay any

Defeat: The Liberal Way of War

After studying hundreds of books written by liberals about the Vietnam War, you realize that their prime objection to this war, waged by liberal presidents John F. Kennedy and Lyndon Baines Johnson, was that it was just too hard to win. They never stepped back and recognized that what made it hard to win was fighting it the liberal way of limited war where you tell the enemy your limits; of graduated response where your carefully calibrate what size of stick is suitable for each enemy infraction—but agree to put the stick away if he'll agree to negotiate; and of general fecklessness compared to an enemy that was willing to destroy their country in order to communize it. Had Richard M. Nixon been elected president in 1960, and had he chosen to fight in Vietnam, he would have won the war—just as he won it, in much tougher conditions, in 1973, only to have the Democrats in Congress abandon our ally and give America's victory away two years later.

price, bear any burden, meet any hardship, support any friend, oppose any foe, in order to assure the survival and the success of liberty."[4] The administration was not alone in this, most of the Kennedy clique felt the same, but it highlighted one of the grubby facts of Kennedy-Johnson foreign policy—that its lofty ideals were often eloquently stated, but there was no real conviction behind them. Johnson had tried to please everyone (Congress, the military, his Democrat constituents, the international community, even the enemy in North Vietnam) and inevitably pleased no one.

The missing (largely successful) years

The drama of the anti-war movement, the Democratic Party's capitulation to it, and the Democratic Congress's scalping of Richard Nixon have overshadowed what happened on the battlefield in Vietnam between 1969 and 1972. On the ground in South Vietnam, General Creighton Abrams (Westmoreland's successor at Military Assistance Command Vietnam, MACV), Ellsworth Bunker (the United States ambassador to South Vietnam from 1969 to 1973), and William Colby (who led the rural pacification efforts), brought the United States an unheralded victory. As the brilliant historian Lewis Sorley points out in his essential volume on this period, *A Better War*, nearly every popular book about Vietnam scarcely addresses the last four years of the war—the years after we had beaten the North Vietnamese on the battlefield, primed the South Vietnamese to take over the war on the ground, and pacified 90 percent of the countryside, while pulling out 100 percent of our combat troops.

Neil Sheehan's 752-page book *A Bright Shining Lie* gives only 65 pages to events after the 1968 Tet Offensive—even though Sheehan's protagonist (John Paul Vann) served another four years in Vietnam after Tet, until his death in a helicopter crash. Vann was an early critic of the American war effort, which is what interests Sheehan. But Vann later changed his opinion, and remarked repeatedly in the latter years of the war that the

United States was clearly winning. Perhaps that's why Sheehan didn't write much about those years. Stanley Karnow's *Vietnam: A History* doesn't get to Tet until page 567 in a 670-page book. George Herring's *America's Longest War* has 60 pages post Tet and 221 pages leading up to it. This pattern is repeated in virtually every history you're likely to find on your public library's bookshelves; most books on the war virtually ignore what are arguably the four most important and successful years of America's involvement with South Vietnam.

Abrams, Bunker, Colby: The team that could

Ambassador Ellsworth Bunker was a patrician Vermonter and a graduate of Yale. He had joined government service after a successful career as a banker and businessman, and was tapped by a succession of presidents for tough diplomatic assignments—including service as ambassador to Brazil, Italy, and India. He was in his early seventies when he was posted to Vietnam in 1967, but he still held his trim body ramrod straight. A Yankee aristocrat of the old school, he was invariably mild-mannered, but exuded the authority of his office and made it clear that he expected disciplined service. He insisted that he be given the facts without bureaucratic gamesmanship, and he brought a clear focus to his duties—he wanted to win the war.[5]

Bunker also brought with him a political maturity and cool management style that contrasted well with the performance of his predecessor, Henry Cabot Lodge, who, aside from winning the ouster of Diem—a pretty hollow victory—had been ineffective in the post. Though Lodge mellowed considerably between his first tour of duty (1963–1964) and his second (1965–1967), the Lodge years were full of internecine strife between the State Department, Defense Department, and the CIA. In contrast, Bunker helped keep everyone on the same page. He liked and respected his team in Vietnam (Abrams on the military side and Colby on the intelligence side) and the mutual admiration was reflected in all they accomplished.

Later, Bunker was asked about the remarkable contrast between the situation in Vietnam in the period 1965 and 1968, during which "as the level of American troops increased, while there was some progress, there was always a sense of frustration," and the years 1969 and 1972, when "as American troops decreased, there seemed to be the considerable sense of momentum and real progress and even élan."[6] Bunker cited improvements in South Vietnam's military, a more effective civil administration, a more stable constitutional framework in South Vietnam, a well-conducted land reform program, and increases in agricultural production. American aide for rural development in South Vietnam was money well spent, and the Americans, civilian and military, who were working to improve the lives of the people, had brought real and beneficial change. Bunker concluded, "I have never served in a more effective organization than the embassy and the military in Vietnam," he concluded.[7]

If Bunker was calm and collected, his military cohort, General Creighton Abrams, was the proverbial dynamo. General Fred Weyand, a corps level commander under General Westmoreland said, "The tactics changed within fifteen minutes of Abrams taking command."[9] Abrams was a West Pointer and a man of well-known integrity. Earthy in expression, no-nonsense, and rock solid, he was a brilliant leader. While he never criticized Westmoreland, after taking command he completely revamped MACV on every count, from sharpening its sense of mission to improving its relationship with the media. The one thing he admired about his enemy was their understanding and complete adherence to the "one war" concept of fighting: the military effort had to be part of a coordinated political and psychological assault on the enemy.

Another Domino Bites the Dust

"American public opinion was the essential domino."[8]

— **Leslie Gelb**, Director of the Pentagon Papers project

Abrams worked to instill that philosophy in his own organization, and succeeded masterfully.

The third member of the team was William E. Colby, a career CIA officer who had begun his career in the Office of Strategic Services (the OSS, the precursor of the CIA) in World War II, parachuting behind German lines. He had once been the CIA's station chief in Saigon. Through a series of diplomatic circumstances involving shifting appointments, he found himself running the rural pacification program in South Vietnam. A bookish-looking man, slight and bespectacled, and a brilliant analyst, he was also highly energetic and fearless. He probably spent more nights in the field among the villagers and ARVN than any other Saigon bureaucrat in the entire war.

Colby's job, fraught with acronyms, euphemisms, and, later, intrigue, had a single objective: to pacify the countryside; or, to put it another way, to remove any reasons for South Vietnamese villagers to be sympathetic to the Communists. To that end, he took on the job of trying to improve the rural economy, eliminate government corruption and harassment, and instill a sense that South Vietnam as an independent entity was worth defending and that Communist propaganda was just that. At the sharp end, he worked to strengthen local defense forces, including making sure they had plentiful supplies of arms—which meant trusting the peasants, something that the government of South Vietnam was sometimes reluctant to do.

Together, these three men, Abrams, Bunker, and Colby—who agreed on the "one war" concept—changed the face of the war.

The old order changeth

In 1969, there were no major Communist attacks. Even the fanatics in Hanoi, having lost an estimated quarter of a million men in 1968, needed a respite.

With the Communists' large military units stopped at the border out of fear of massive American firepower, Abrams directed his commanders to use small units to seek and destroy the enemy within South Vietnam. Unlike the earlier large scale search and destroy missions, however, the units were to search, destroy, and hold, clearing out the enemy so that Colby's pacification program could take over. Abrams kept up continuous pressure on the Viet Cong and NVA. Historian and soldier Dave Richard Palmer quotes one American general who said it was like windshield wiper tactics: "We just keep going, going, going back and forth to keep the countryside clear."[10]

Colby supervised the building of village and regional defenses. He and his men armed the villagers and instructed them in the basics of small unit combat, fortification, and intelligence gathering. Over the next three years, half a million weapons were given to South Vietnamese villagers. Colby was unworried that these weapons might go to the enemy. As he said, the Communists had plenty of—and far superior—weapons of their own; and in tracking the weapons he doled out, he found that the loss rate was only 2 or 3 percent. The key point, Colby said, was to show the villagers that the government had confidence in them.[11]

Colby and Abrams agreed that intelligence gathering and interpretation had to be improved. And it was. In 1969, a Communist cryptographer defected to South Vietnam. He brought with him a vast catalogue of plans, outlook reports, and strategic papers issued by COSVN, the Central Office for South Vietnam—the command center of the Communist Party of the southern half of South Vietnam (thought to be headquartered in Cambodia for most of the war). This was a coup, but Colby went farther than merely analyzing the data. The need for better intelligence led to the most controversial aspect of his pacification efforts—the Phoenix program.

The Phoenix program

President Thieu initiated the Phoenix program in 1967 as an effort to understand, so as to be able to combat, the Viet Cong/Communist infrastructure operating in South Vietnam. What was known was that the Viet Cong, numbering in the thousands of men, exercised considerable control over portions of the rural populace through intimidation, coercion, and armed assaults. What was not known was how they operated, how they gathered intelligence, how they passed that intelligence from village to village and up to COSVN.

It was put on hold during the Tet Offensive, when the priority became caring for refugees and rebuilding what had been destroyed. In 1968, however, it was reinstated thanks to Colby's efforts in bringing together Vietnamese and American intelligence agencies and arranging for American advisors to join the program to work with the local Vietnamese officials, military, police, and civilians. President Thieu readily agreed and signed a new decree in July 1968, establishing the revised Phoenix program as a national priority. Phoenix centers were to be placed in each of the country's 244 administrative districts. Each district was to contribute its knowledge of the local Viet Cong infrastructure (VCI) and activities.

It was easily the most controversial part of the pacification program run by Colby in his time in Vietnam. "One decision about the program was made at the outset: that it would not be a secret police activity."[12] Colby worried that the program might be misrepresented as being somehow illicit or immoral. He published a Command Directive (reproduced here) to make clear to the Vietnamese and Americans the rules and limitations concerning their activities.

> The PHOENIX program is one of advice, support and assistance to the GVN Phuong Hoang program, aimed at reducing the influence and effectiveness of the Viet Cong Infrastructure in South Vietnam. The Viet Cong Infrastructure is an inherent

part of the war effort being waged against the GVN by the Viet Cong and their North Vietnamese Allies. The unlawful status of members of the Viet Cong Infrastructure (as defined in the Green Book and in GVN official decrees) is well established in GVN law and is in full accord with the laws of land warfare followed by the United States Army.

Operations against the Viet Cong Infrastructure include the collection of intelligence identifying these members, inducing them to abandon their allegiance to the Viet Cong and rally to the government, capturing or arresting them in order to bring them before Province Security Committees for lawful sentencing, and, as a last resort, the use of military or police force against them if no other way of preventing them from carrying on their unlawful activities is possible. Our training emphasizes the desirability of obtaining these target individuals alive and of using intelligent and lawful methods of interrogation to obtain the truth of what they know about other aspects of the Viet Cong Infrastructure. U.S. personnel are under the same legal and moral constraints with respect to operations of a Phoenix character as they are with respect to regular military operations against enemy units in the field. Thus, they are specifically not authorized to engage in assassinations or other violations of the rules of land warfare, but they are entitled to use such reasonable military force as is necessary to obtain the goals of rallying, capturing, or eliminating the Viet Cong Infrastructure in the Republic of Viet-Nam.

If U.S. personnel come in contact with activities conducted by Vietnamese which do not meet the standard rules of land warfare, they are certainly not to participate further in the activity. They are also expected to make their objections to this kind of behavior known to the Vietnamese conducting them and they are expected to report the circumstances to next higher U.S. authority for decision as to action to be taken with the GVN. (There follows a paragraph which allows for U.S. military assigned to Phoenix to opt out of the program without prejudice).

Those who knew Bill Colby, as I did, well understood that he meant each and every word. He wrote the directive in plain English, without euphemisms. Nevertheless, the Phoenix Program became, and to a great extent remains, in the public mind, a "synonym" for assassination, torture, and brutality by the government of South Vietnam and the United States. The reasons, to an extent, are easily understood:

There was confusion about the programs for *intelligence* gathering, the function of the Phoenix program, and the function of the local defense units which ran *operations* against the Viet Cong in conventional battles and skirmishes. Operations forces were everyone from the regular army to the self-defense militia. They used the Phoenix intelligence, but were not part of the program. Most of the Viet Cong killed were the result of standard military operations.

Still, it was not unknown for intelligence operatives, who had suffered the loss through death or kidnapping of a relative by the Viet Cong, to act outside of the rules of the intelligence unit when a Viet Cong operative was exposed, especially when the Viet Cong might have been directly involved in the murder or kidnapping.

And, of course, it was easily believed and reported by news media that the intelligence functions of Phoenix, being CIA operations (by association with Bill Colby, who was technically an employee of U.S.AID at the time he was running the program), knowingly operated outside the boundaries of legality. A great many liberal reporters made the assumption that if the CIA was involved, it must be something evil, though Colby was himself a liberal—albeit one of that rare breed who kept faith with the South Vietnamese and believed not only that the war could have been won but was.

By the end of October 1969, the Accelerated Pacification Program, under the command of General Abrams, operated by William Colby, had reached and in fact exceeded its goals for the year. Ninety-two percent of the people in the countryside were now living in category A, B, or C hamlets, meaning "relatively secure." Traffic on the roads was near normal except in known areas of VC concentra-

> ## And for What?
>
> Former Viet Cong Colonel Pham Xuan An had an embittered answer: "All that talk about 'liberation' twenty, thirty, forty years ago, all the plotting, and all the bodies, produced this, this impoverished, broken-down country led by a gang of cruel and paternalistic half-educated theorists."[14]

tions. Life was beginning to be as normal as could be expected living in a country under siege by Communists.

Even the enemy conceded the program's effectiveness, noting that the pacification program "combined political, economic, and cultural schemes with espionage warfare in order to eliminate the infrastructure of the revolution."[13] Exactly what it was meant to do.

Writer and historian Stanley Karnow was skeptical of the Phoenix program until he met with North Vietnamese leaders after the war. "The Communist authorities in Vietnam ... said that Phoenix was the 'single most effective program that you used against them in the entire war.'"[15]

The handoff to Nixon—no more Mr. Nice Guy

After the collapse of the Tet Offensive, Hanoi's Communists scooted to Moscow pleading for help. They got it. Within a short time, Giap was able to equip and send six or seven new divisions of NVA freshly supplied troops south, taking the place of the Viet Cong who had been wiped out during Tet.

President Johnson, meanwhile, was neck-deep in success but didn't know it. His administration, used to having the media on its side for the Great Society, was gutted by the rumbling criticism from the liberal media that became a full-fledged roar after the Tet Offensive. LBJ, tired, media-harried, and sniped at by his own party, threw in the towel, announcing he would not run for reelection in 1968. Unfortunately for the troops in the field, Johnson had no more idea of how to disengage from a limited war than he knew how to fight one. The United States had 525,000 men in Vietnam. What should they do?

LBJ never directly answered that question. He left it to his successor, Republican Richard M. Nixon, who loathed the media and knew the feeling was mutual. He had a plan for Vietnam. He called it "peace with honor." His secretary of state saw it as applying the principles of *Realpolitik* (dealing with the actual situation to further America's national interests, rather than operating by theory, like former administrations) to the war in Vietnam. The plan was both ambitious and humble. Nixon disdained Kennedy's rhetoric of carrying the torch of liberty around the world. He spoke in terms of America's national interests. He intended to support our allies, but they would have to provide their own manpower to fight their wars—we wouldn't do it for them. To that end, Nixon began a process of "Vietnamization"—a rapid but well-executed transfer of responsibility from the United States military to the military of South Vietnam. He was audacious in working to widen the divide between North Vietnam's two great patrons, China and Russia. He disdained the ineffective doctrine of "graduated response" that had guided the Johnson administration in favor of a 1970s version of short bouts of military "shock and awe," which startled and worried the North Vietnamese government. Reviled, laughed at, cursed, and dismissed by the intelligentsia, Nixon was decisive where Kennedy waffled; and he was a tough-minded statesman while Johnson was an

Peace with Honor

Just after his inauguration, Nixon said: "When we assumed the burden of helping defend South Vietnam, millions of South Vietnamese men, women, and children placed their trust in us. To abandon them now would risk a massacre.... Abandoning the South Vietnamese people...would threaten our long-term hopes for peace in the world. A great nation cannot renege on its pledges. A great nation must be worthy of trust.... If we simply abandoned our effort in Vietnam, the cause of peace might not survive the damage that would be done to other nations' confidence in our reliability.... If Hanoi were to succeed in taking over South Vietnam by force—even after the power of the United States had been engaged—it would greatly strengthen those leaders who scorn negotiation, who advocate aggression, who minimize the risks of confrontation with the United States. It would bring peace now, but it would enormously increase the danger of a bigger war."[16] One wonders which part the liberal anti-war activists didn't understand.

over-promoted congressional enforcer. Nixon succeeded where his Democratic predecessors (and political opponents) failed.

At his inauguration on January 20, 1969, Nixon spoke of being a peace-maker. Five days later, the Paris peace talks opened; that was the carrot. On March 17, 1969, Nixon applied the stick, authorizing Operation Menu, the bombing of Cambodia, targeting the North Vietnamese supply sanctuaries located along the border.

In May, Nixon called for a simultaneous withdrawal of American and North Vietnamese forces from South Vietnam. Hanoi refused and repeated its demands that the Viet Cong, no longer a force to reckon with, become a part of a coalition government in South Vietnam—a demand the North Vietnamese themselves ignored when they conquered South Vietnam six years later and offered no meaningful position to any Viet Cong representative in the new government.

In July, Nixon announced that the United States would provide military and economic assistance to nations combating Communism, but would not commit ground troops (what became known as the Nixon Doctrine). His administration drew up plans for a graduated withdrawal of American troops from Vietnam, the process to be completed by the end of 1972—a deadline that Nixon achieved—and Nixon put down a marker by withdrawing 100,000 troops in 1969.

The so-called Peace Movement was neither impressed nor appeased: in part because it was impossible for it to praise a man like Nixon, in part because a hard cadre of anti-war leaders and protesters were openly in favor of the Communists (and the Communist government of North Vietnam was openly in favor of the protesters), and in part because when the North Vietnamese proved intransigent at the negotiating table, Nixon responded with the sort of force that LBJ had shied away from.

By the end of 1969, peace negotiations were deadlocked. The Communists so frustrated Ambassador Lodge, America's chief negotiator at the Paris peace talks, that he resigned. Hanoi saw the withdrawals of American troops, snickered at the notion that the ARVN could ever withstand the NVA, noted the anti-war mood of the Democratic Congress, and cheered the demonstrations of the so-called peace activists. They saw no reason to negotiate. Victory was in the offing.

What the Communists in Hanoi didn't anticipate was Nixon's tenacity.

Ever since taking command, General Abrams had wanted permission to send Allied troops into Cambodia—for reconnaissance, if nothing else. "The authority requested, we realize," Abrams acknowledged in 1968, "is much greater than anyone has asked for in the past...[however]...Partial measures will not suffice."[17] The request was denied by the Johnson administration. Abrams then asked for permission to bomb enemy forces in Cambodia. In the spring of 1969, the Nixon administration approved his request. It marked the true beginning of Nixon's war.

The "secret" bombing

North Vietnam had occupied eastern Cambodia for four years, using it as a safe haven to stockpile troops and supplies, confident that the United States had no desire to expand the war in Indochina. For the NVA, Cambodia was a refuge from American fire-power, a sanctuary to which it could always flee. According to North Vietnamese accounts, up to 300,000 North Vietnamese soldiers were quartered and equipped in Cambodia in 1969–1970. The vast majority of these soldiers were combat troops; and there they sat, un-harassed in a "neutral" country no more than five miles from the border of South Vietnam.

And then the North Vietnamese provided another provocation.

In 1968, the Johnson administration had reached an unwritten understanding with Hanoi that there would be no North Vietnamese attacks on South Vietnamese cities during the peace negotiations.[18] Nevertheless, on February 22, 1969, Hanoi launched a countrywide offensive in South Vietnam. Enraged, Nixon asked the chiefs of staff of the armed forces for an appropriate response—even while he conceded that liberal opinion-makers both at home and abroad would be unstinting in their vitriol against him if he retaliated.

The North Vietnamese offensive drove American casualties to four hundred killed per week. In a news conference on March 4, 1969, Nixon said, "We will not tolerate a continuation of a violation of an understanding. But more than that, we will not tolerate attacks which result in heavier casualties to our men at a time that we are honestly trying to seek peace at the conference table in Paris. An appropriate response to these attacks will be made if they continue."[19]

Still, Nixon held off. After issuing an order to start bombing the Cambodian sanctuaries on 9 March, he retracted the order, with advice and counsel from, among others, his secretary of state William Rogers. But after five North Vietnamese rockets hit Saigon—the thirty-second attack on a South Vietnamese city in two weeks—Nixon decided he had to attack North Vietnam's Cambodian sanctuaries. On 16 March, Nixon met in the Oval Office with the Secretaries of Defense (Melvin Laird) and State (William Rogers), the Chairman of the Joint Chiefs of Staff (General Earle Wheeler), and National Security Advisor Henry Kissinger. Although he had made up his mind to go forward with the bombing, Nixon felt he should meet with his top advisors prior to any action.

The Sunday afternoon meeting went on for hours. Secretary Rogers objected to the action on domestic grounds (particularly the negative reaction anticipated in Congress). Laird and Wheeler thought the bombing should go forward. Cambodia's alleged neutral status was not discussed. According to Kissinger, "It was taken for granted that we had the right to counter North Vietnam's blatant violation of Cambodia's neutrality since Cambodia was unwilling or unable to defend its neutral status."[21] Nixon's view was that the operation was soundly based in International Law, specifically the Hague Convention of 1907: "A neutral country has the obligation not to allow its territory to be used by a belligerent. If the neutral country is unwilling or unable to prevent this, the other belligerent has the right to take appropriate counteraction."[22]

Diplomacy at Home

Nixon was not always gracious in his statements and demeanor with regard to his adversaries in Congress. After his "silent majority" speech urging Americans to be "united for peace" (which initially worked very well, as most Americans approved his handling of the war), Nixon boasted, "We've got those liberal bastards on the run, and we're going to keep them on the run."[20]

Kissinger noted, "These deliberations are instructive: A month of an unprovoked North Vietnamese offensive, over a thousand Americans dead, elicited after weeks of anguished discussion exactly *one* American retaliatory raid within three miles of the Cambodian border in an area occupied by the North Vietnamese for over four years. And this would enter the folklore as an example of wanton 'illegality.'"[23] It was also later criticized for its alleged secrecy.

Nixon ordered the bombing mission to proceed, and on 18 March, a B-52 attack was carried out against a target designated as Base Area 353. More than 2,000 tons of bombs were dropped on what was presumed to be the location of COSVN. A total of seventy-three secondary explosions were reported, the clear sign that ammunitions stored on the ground had been hit.

There was no reaction of any kind—from Hanoi, Phnom Penh, Moscow, or Peking. Neither North Vietnam nor Cambodia ever claimed there were any civilian casualties. Given the intensity of the bombing, it is likely that there *were* civilian casualties, but not anywhere close to the 600,000 (or even 100,000) that some anti-war activists claimed were the result of America's bombing campaign against Communist targets in Cambodia. Eastern Cambodia was not heavily populated. Moreover, the North Vietnamese did not want Cambodian peasants near their camps, except as labor and later for conscription, and few people, if they have the choice, want to live near a war zone.

The alleged "secrecy" of the bombing was a misnomer. Certainly Nixon did not announce it publicly; but since when do military plans have to be divulged to the enemy? If the United States had announced the bombing, Sihanouk would have been in an awkward position, having secretly agreed to the operation, and the North Vietnamese would not only have been alerted, but perhaps have been prompted to launch a counteroffensive to save face. A full briefing on the results of the campaign was given in the Oval Office on June 11, 1969, to House and Senate leaders, including Senator John Stennis (chairman of the Senate Armed Services Committee), Senator Richard Russell (chairman of the Senate Appropriations Committee), Senator Everett Dirksen, Congressman Mendel Rivers (chairman of the House Armed Services Committee), Congressman Leslie Arends, and Congressman Gerald Ford (the House minority leader). No one suggested briefing the entire Congress.

During the bombing, even the pilots weren't given their targets until the last minute. But within weeks of the first "secret" bombing of the Cambodian sanctuaries, every major news outlet in the United States, including the *New York Times,* the *Washington Post,* UPI, and the *Wall Street Journal* carried stories, some detailed, of the bombing of Cambodia. So much for secrets.

The Cambodian "Invasion"

According to any number of leftists, President Nixon's approval of a three-month incursion against North Vietnamese sanctuaries in Cambodia qualifies him as the "century's worst war criminal" and guilty of "genocide."[24]

As usual, they're wrong—grotesquely wrong.

In April 1970, Nixon announced to the United States and the world that he was authorizing American military incursions into Cambodia (the South Vietnamese would join in). As the United States continued its drawdown of troops, he knew it was too dangerous to allow the enemy to continue to build resources and strength just across the border of Vietnam. Also the Khmer Rouge, Cambodian Communists, had been making gains against Lon Nol, the ruler-by-coup of Cambodia, turning an allegedly "neutral" country a deeper shade of Communist red.

It cannot be stated too often: *The purpose of the Cambodian incursion was to eliminate Communist sanctuaries, encourage Hanoi to negotiate a peace, and better secure South Vietnam's eastern border so that American troops could withdraw from the country more easily.* But to anti-war lib-erals, whose protests swept across America, Nixon was hugely expanding the war, and by intervening against the Communists in Cambodia, he allegedly, in one of the wildest and yet most accepted flights of fancy of Nixon's critics, destabilized the country, ensuring the triumph of the Khmer Rouge. They might as well blame Nixon for Original Sin, too.

The fact is that while the ultra-mercurial leader of Cambodia, Prince Norodom Sihanouk, tried to maintain a façade of neutrality, he faced a future, and indeed the present, as a de facto North Vietnamese satellite state. That was why the Cambodian army, such as it was, took no action against the North Vietnamese Army that occupied eastern Cambodia. It is also why he granted the NVA the right to use the port at Sihanoukville for shipments of military supplies (allegedly, Communist bribes helped ensure this policy). On the other hand, he was *not* a Communist—indeed, he said he hated the Communists—and did not protest when the United States intervened in Cambodia. He had concluded, though, that the Com-munists would win in Southeast Asia. This put him in the odd position of being an uneasy and unreliable ally of the United States who simulta-neously aligned himself with China and by association with the North Vietnamese, whom he allowed to occupy vast swathes of his country.

Some of his subjects, however, were rather more vigorous in their anti-Communism. In March 1970, while he was visiting France, Sihanouk was overthrown by Prime Minister Lon Nol, who invited the United States to help him rid Cambodia of the "occupying" Communist army. Sihanouk, exiled in China, allied himself with the Communist Khmer Rouge, a com-plicated offshoot of the Indochina Communist Party, and became the nominal head of a Khmer Rouge government-in-exile. Many people, espe-cially in rural areas, maintained a sense of loyalty to Prince Sihanouk, and this increased the political appeal of the Khmer Rouge, which waged war against the Lon Nol government. By 1973, the Khmer Rouge effec-tively controlled much of the countryside; rural Cambodians believed that by supporting the Khmer Rouge, they were actually supporting the return of Sihanouk.

The Khmer Rouge was founded in the 1920s with help from Ho Chi Minh. Its leader, Pol Pot, was well-trained in Maoist doctrine, and absolutely lacked mercy or regard for his fellow Cambodian citizens as people. Everything was subverted to the ideology of Maoist revolution and class warfare. It began to create problems for the Cambodian government in the last half of the 1960s, though at that point it had only a few thousand men under arms. In 1968, however, the Khmer Rouge forces launched a national insurgency across Cambodia. North Vietnam forces provided shelter and weapons to the Khmer Rouge. For the next two years, the insurgency grew as Sihanouk did very little to stop it. After Sihanouk's ouster, Lon Nol tried to rid Cambodia of this new Communist threat, but North Vietnamese support for the insurgency made it impossible for the Cambodian military to counter it.

In 1970, Richard Nixon faced the likely establishment of a Communist Cambodia, with North Vietnamese troops forming up along an 800-mile border with South Vietnam. Nixon's goal in sending American troops into Cambodia was not to "widen the war" as his critics

Reeducation Camps: Kum-Ba-Yah Around the Camp Fire?

The best estimates are that the North Vietnamese sent 250,000 people to Reeducation Camps after their victory in 1975. Writer Nguyen Van Canh probably said it best:

"The notion that torture, summary execution, deprivation of medical care, or slow death from malnutrition are likely to improve anyone's attitude toward the government that inflicts them upon him is one that even a communist theoretician would not attempt to make plausible."[25]

proclaimed in shrill and hysterical denunciations of the president, but to guard South Vietnam's left flank, to protect American troops, to shore up Lon Nol in his fight against the Communists, and to prevent a widening enemy front that might endanger his rapidly progressing policy of "Vietnamization." American units were coming home at a swift pace, with the South Vietnamese army taking over more and more responsibility for fighting the Communists. Nixon's incursion into Cambodia was meant to secure South Vietnam's eastern border so that the process could continue and maintain its rapid pace. Nixon knew he would catch holy political hell for his action; he knew anti-war protestors would launch a frenzy of protests; but he did it anyway, because he believed it was the right and necessary thing to do.

Colonel Charles Askins of the United States Army, who first went to Vietnam in the 1950s, and who knew Sihanouk, was asked about Nixon's decision to send American troops into Cambodia in 1970. His response: "For the Commander in Chief to *not* use every means of protecting the troops would have gotten him kicked out of office in any country with common sense. I don't care if he did it because he was paranoid, insecure, or dead drunk, he made the right decision. If a military leader sacrificed the safety of his men just to keep some jackass from burning down the ROTC building in Padooka, I'd shoot him myself."[26]

By the latter part of April 1970, Lon Nol's position was rapidly deteriorating. The North Vietnamese had continued to push west into Cambodia and were threatening the capitol, Phnom Penh. In discussions at the White House, Nixon, Kissinger, and the military were for striking against the Communists in Cambodia; Nixon's civilian advisors were generally opposed. At a National Security Council meeting on April 22, 1970, Nixon decided that the South Vietnamese should attack NVA sanctuaries in an area known as the "Parrot's Beak" in eastern Cambodia. They would be supported as necessary by the United States Air Force. The more difficult decision, using American ground troops, was put off for a few more days of discussion. All of the participating advisors, and the president, were aware of the domestic risks. General Abrams, the senior American military man in South Vietnam, advised the president that he could not assure success in the Cambodian venture unless he could use American troops. On 28 April, Nixon made the final decision that South Vietnamese forces would attack the Parrot's Beak and American troops would assault the "Fish Hook" some fifty to sixty miles farther north.

On D-Day, May 1, 1970, 15,000 Americans attacked, preceded by B-52 raids and supported by tanks. The enemy fled west, and no great battles ensued. To the south, the day before, nearly 8,000 ARVN troops had attacked the Parrot's Beak. After a few early skirmishes, they too found that the NVA had fled. The enemy, however, lost more than 12,000 soldiers killed and another thousand-plus captured. The Americans suffered 434 dead and 2,233 wounded.[27]

Captured arms and ammunition gave proof of the danger of allowing the NVA a sanctuary in Cambodia. More than 23,000 weapons were captured (enough to equip 74 NVA battalions), along with 2,500 crew-served weapons, 16 million rounds of small arms ammunition (one year's worth of ammunition for the Communists), 14 million pounds of rice, 143,000 rounds of mortar, rocket, and recoilless rifle ammunition, and about 200,000 rounds of anti-aircraft ammunition.[28]

The Communist pressure on Lon Nol was temporarily relieved, giving him time to try to buildup his forces. Sir Robert Thompson, the British counter-insurgency expert, estimated that the ARVN-American invasion, limited as it was, set the NVA timetable back 18 to 24 months. The ARVN gained confidence in their ability to fight and defeat the NVA, and by protecting South Vietnam's left flank, American troops could continue their orderly departure from the country.

In the United States, this alleged "widening of the war" caused an explosion of protests on college campuses, including the killing of four students by poorly trained, nervous, and scared Ohio National Guardsmen

at Kent State on May 4, 1970. Often forgotten was that the "Kent State Massacre"
was preceded by days of violent rioting
(including the burning of the ROTC building), reaching its climax on May 4, and
that the troops, already under attack by a
rock-throwing mob, fired only after one of
the radicals pistol-whipped another student and then charged, pointed gun in
hand, at the guardsmen. Tragically, two of
the killed were innocent bystanders, one
of whom, in fact, was enrolled in ROTC.

He Who Hesitates Is Lost

"The bane of our military actions in Vietnam was the hesitancy [of those actions]; we were always trying to calculate with fine precision the absolute minimum of force or of time, leaving no margin for error or confusion, encouraging our adversary to hold on until our doubts over-rode our efforts."[29]

Despite hundreds of campus protests,
the closing down of scores of universities,
and the condemnation of the press, a Gallup poll soon after the Cambodian incursion showed Nixon with no serious drop in his popularity. Less
than two years later he would be reelected to a second term by a record-
setting majority. Common sense still prevailed in America's heartland.

Throughout the summer and fall of 1970, Nixon repeatedly warned
Hanoi that if it continued its attacks on South Vietnam (and on Cambodia), he might authorize more bombing raids against North Vietnam. The
North Vietnamese, perhaps encouraged by the anti-war protests roiling
American college campuses and by the efforts by Democrats in Congress
to limit Nixon's power, remained aggressive. They pushed toward Phnom
Penh in Cambodia only to be driven back by American air power. They
maintained more than 40,000 troops in Laos. They did not curtail their
attacks on South Vietnam.

In the spring of 1970, the United States Senate voted to repeal the Gulf
of Tonkin Resolution (the appeal became law in 1971); Congress followed
up in December 1970 with an amendment to the defense authorizations
bill that forbade American ground forces from conducting operations in

Laos or Cambodia. Nixon and Kissinger found themselves not only fighting the enemy abroad but confronting a hostile Congress at home that was intent on handcuffing the commander in chief. In October 1970, Nixon proposed a cease-fire until a formal peace agreement could be reached. But Hanoi viewed this only as another sign of weakening American will and did not respond. Moreover, time appeared on Hanoi's side, as American troops continued their steady withdrawal. By the end 1970, Nixon had cut America's troop levels in Vietnam by roughly one half since his inauguration in January 1969.

Despite all the political forces working against him, Nixon believed that Vietnamization was working, that "peace with honor" would soon be achieved. On January 4, 1971, he assured the American people that "The end [of the war] is in sight."[30] Lest the North Vietnamese take any comfort in that announcement, the United States launched heavy airstrikes against NVA supply camps in Laos and Cambodia. It was obvious that the Nixon administration believed that a key to securing peace in Vietnam was denying the enemy sanctuaries in Laos and Cambodia.

Nixon delivers

A test of Vietnamization was launched on January 30, 1971, with an all-Vietnamese ground offensive into Laos. Seventeen thousand ARVN attacked 22,000 NVA inside Laos in an attempt to cut the Ho Chi Minh trail. The Operation, Lam Son 719, was supported by U.S. artillery, air strikes, and helicopter support that ferried ARVN troops into combat. The fighting did not go well. Tough terrain and bad weather kept the ARVN from reaching their objectives on schedule, and the delay allowed the NVA to bring 20,000 troops to the battle. The ARVN suffered more than 7,500 casualties—almost half of the invasion force. The press was on hand to witness the scrambling, panicked retreat of the ARVN. They proclaimed it as proof that Nixon's Vietnamization program was failure. The

ARVN had certainly performed poorly. But it was also true that as many as 20,000 North Vietnamese had been killed or wounded (thanks to American air support). So the battle was not exactly a disaster for the Americans and South Vietnamese (the United States had lost 200 killed, along with 100 helicopters downed and another 600 damaged). The lesson Nixon took away from the battle was not that Vietnamization was a failure, but that American air power, much maligned because of its failure to bomb Hanoi into submission earlier in the war, could ensure its success. Whenever the NVA concentrated their forces for a decisive attack, they would be vulnerable to American air strikes. In short, the United States could ensure South Vietnam's independence without having to keep any significant number of troops on the ground.

Indeed, on the field of battle, the North Vietnamese continued to take a beating—so much so that on March 10, 1971, Communist China thought

You Say Invasion and I Say Incursion

The anti-war protesters who were so furious over the Cambodian "invasion," which was a legal incursion into an enemy sanctuary in a neutral country lasting a few weeks, ignored the North Vietnamese invasion of South Vietnam, which was an illegal invasion—a war—that lasted more than a decade. Go figure. "Expanding the war" was another one of the Left's headline-grabbing rallying cries, but it did not reflect the truth of the Cambodian incursion. The fact was the United States was not "expanding" the war—it was striking the same enemy, for the same reasons, and doing so to end the war in a way that would preserve the independence of the internationally recognized sovereign state of South Vietnam.

it needed to make a public announcement of its full support for North Vietnam. Nixon was proving a tenacious foe. At home, he continued to face down a hostile Congress, an even more hostile media, and the biggest anti-war demonstrations since the Civil War; in Southeast Asia, he was deftly withdrawing American troops while hammering the enemy to agree to a negotiated peace.

In June 1971, the *New York Times* published what it thought might be a devastating blow to Nixon—the "Pentagon Papers." These were a compilation (which McNamara had ordered to be assembled in 1967) of classified documents about why the United States had entered the war and how the war had been conducted. The Nixon administration went to the courts to try to halt further publication of classified documents, but less than a week later, the *Washington Post* began publishing the Pentagon Papers, in what was seen as a battle to preserve the First Amendment— though Nixon rightly assumed that real motivation was to provide ammunition to the anti-war cause. The newspaper spin was that the papers presented the lies, deceptions, mistakes, and misjudgments that had led America into Indochina, and that this was why the Nixon administration had tried to block their publication. In fact, if you actually read the papers, you find that far from revealing lies and deception, they show how the United States had entered the Vietnam War full of (old-style) liberal idealism. Apparently, in their frenzy to discredit the war, the media didn't seem bothered by this. It was President Nixon, the man defeated by Kennedy in the 1960 presidential election, who, de facto, was fighting to preserve the reputations of the Kennedy and Johnson administrations—indeed, he was at that very moment trying to pull their chestnuts out of the fire with his program of Vietnamization. Of course, to him, the real issue about the Pentagon Papers was that secret information, such as the papers contained, should not be leaked to the enemy—and certainly not in a time of war.

If Nixon felt besieged by domestic enemies, perhaps it was because he was. On June 22, 1971, a non-binding resolution was passed in the U.S. Senate urging the removal of all American troops from Vietnam within six months. Senator Mike Mansfield called the war "a tragic mistake." On June 30, the U.S. Supreme Court ruled 6 to 3 in favor of the *New York Times* and the *Washington Post* in the Pentagon Papers case.

But just when it seemed that Nixon might be on the ropes, he made a stunning diplomatic pronouncement. On July 15, 1971, President Nixon announced that he would visit Communist China in February. One might assume that the shock in Hanoi was equal to the shock in Washington. Nixon showed that this masterstroke of diplomacy would not weaken his prosecution of the war in Vietnam. In December, just weeks ahead of his trip to Peking, Nixon authorized heavy bombing of military installations in North Vietnam.

Thanks, Democratic Congress!

"Let us understand: North Vietnam cannot defeat or humiliate the United States. Only Americans can do that."

—Richard M. Nixon, 1969

Nixon's trip to China was one of the most startling diplomatic developments of the twentieth century. He met with Chairman Mao Tse-Tung and Prime Minister Chou En-lai over the course of a weeklong visit, from February 21 to February 28, 1972. Moscow worried that the United States was going to widen the Sino-Soviet rift to America's advantage. Hanoi—although by now almost totally reliant on Russian support and arms to prosecute its aggression in South Vietnam—worried that the Chinese might press North Vietnam to settle for a peace the Vietnamese Communists didn't want; and there were also fears that Communist China might forget Communist solidarity and actually turn against Hanoi. At the very least, Nixon's visit began a Cold War thaw in Asia and unnerved North Vietnam.

In the meantime, Nixon continued his strategy of winding down the war. The famed 101st Airborne Division departed Vietnam on March 10, 1972. The last of the combat Marines had departed a year earlier. But American airpower continued to devastate Giap's army whenever it exposed itself for another attack—and attacking was Hanoi's consistent alternative to negotiating in Paris.

Giap decided on one last throw of the dice. He knew that Communist China was pushing Hanoi to negotiate, but he also knew that Nixon was

The Genius of NVA General Vo Nguyen Giap

Widely held as a military genius (one publication called him the most important military leader of the twentieth century),[42] Giap's strategic rules might be broken down thus:

1. Have an unlimited supply of cannon fodder; ten to twenty percent of your country's population might suffice.
2. Have hundreds of thousands of coolies to build infrastructure without paying overtime or, in fact, even paying.
3. Have all the time in the world and nothing else to do.
4. Have an unlimited supply of—free! free! free!—weapons, ammunition, and vehicles delivered to your doorstep by indulgent friends—(oh, and have the doorstep off-limits from enemy attack).
5. Have the chutzpah to stand knee-deep in your troops' gore and mangled limbs and declare a victory; in fact declare it was your plan all along to win a war of attrition that you actually lost.
6. Have the "underdog" status so world opinion stays on your side.
7. Have the ability to control the press—your own and the enemy's. (Okay, the latter took some strategy.)

up for reelection. Perhaps a major North Vietnamese offensive would push Nixon from the White House as Tet had pushed Johnson. In March 30, 1972, Giap launched his Easter Offensive, sending 200,000 North Vietnamese soldiers south in an all out attempt to conquer South Vietnam.

The North Vietnamese army besieged and captured the city of Quang Tri (in northern South Vietnam), tried to cut South Vietnam in half with a major assault against the city of Kontum (in central South Vietnam), and attacked An Loc (in the south). Nixon responded by authorizing the

8. Have the ability to articulate your strategy as below (from *How We Won the War* by Giap):

"In choosing the directions and targets for our attacks we correctly aimed at the vital points of the enemy. These vital points were in most cases places where the enemy was weak or relatively weak. These might also be places where they were strong or relatively strong. But in both cases, the enemy was exposed or relatively exposed, this situation being created either through the enemy's own fault or by our action. There we had the necessary conditions to muster an overpowering force, deal surprise blows, use effective combat methods and knock the enemy out rapidly." [43]

(Exactly! Dodge those non-vital points and hit the enemy where he is either weak or strong. Why didn't we think of that?)

9. Have an enemy with morals and conscience publish its "Rules of Engagement."

10. Have a pirated copy of *Barbarella* to blackmail movie stars to your support.

United States 7th Fleet to target NVA troops massed around the DMZ with air strikes and naval gunfire. Then he gave the go-ahead for a massive bombing attack targeting all NVA troops in South Vietnam, along with B-52 strikes against North Vietnam. "The bastards have never been bombed like they're going to be bombed this time," he said to Kissinger.[31] The bombing included Hanoi and Haiphong harbor. Nixon ramped up the counterstrike with Operation Linebacker I—the mining of North Vietnam's harbors along with intensified bombing of North Vietnamese roads, bridges, and oil facilities.

At this point, there were only 69,000 American troops in South Vietnam, fewer than a third of those were combat troops, and despite all the bombing Nixon had authorized, even American air power had been significantly drawn down to the point that the United States was scrambling to field combat aircraft. Still, Nixon was counting on absolute air superiority along with the guns of the 7th Fleet to help the ARVN repel the North Vietnamese invasion.

In May, Nixon began chopping at another leg of Hanoi's wobbling stool. Meeting in Moscow with Leonid Brezhnev, Nixon discussed improving American-Soviet diplomatic relations. The Soviet Union supplied Hanoi with 90 percent of its war material. The North Vietnamese could not be happy. They were being diplomatically isolated—and the battlefield results weren't looking very good either.

Aided by massive U.S. air strikes, the ARVN beat back the attack on Kontum. American naval gunfire and B-52 bombardments supported the ARVN as they recaptured Quang Tri. By mid-July the NVA, shredded by B-52 bombing runs, gave up attacking An Loc. Nixon did not let up. On September 29, the United States struck North Vietnamese airfields, destroying ten percent of Hanoi's air force.

In Paris, Hanoi finally appeared willing to negotiate. On October 8, 1972, Henry Kissinger and Le Duc Tho reached a compromise draft settlement. The United States agreed to allow North Vietnamese troops already in

South Vietnam to remain there (a major concession and one that incensed South Vietnam's government) and North Vietnam, in exchange, dropped its demand that there could be no peace accord until South Vietnam's President Nguyen van Thieu resigned and his government was dissolved. Kissinger gambled that the threat of U.S. airpower would prevent the North Vietnamese from mounting a significant offensive after a treaty. South Vietnam, in the meantime, could continue improving its own armed forces and securing the countryside. The recent successes of the ARVN at Kontum, Quang Tri, and An Loc, gave some hope that Vietnamization was beginning to work. During the Easter Offensive, the NVA lost upwards of 100,000 troops, half its tanks and artillery, and the hero of Dien Bien Phu, General Giap, was relieved of command of the army.

Whining Doesn't Get It Done

"One reason the Kennedy and Johnson administrations failed to take an orderly, rational approach to the basic questions underlying Vietnam was the staggering variety and complexity of other issues we faced. Simply put, we faced a blizzard of problems, there were only twenty-four hours in a day, and we often did not have time to think straight."

—**Robert S. McNamara**[32]

Did it ever occur to this whining genius to just stick with the basics? Win the damn war.

The tide appeared to be changing. On November 7, 1972, Richard M. Nixon won reelection by the biggest landslide in American history, besting a Democratic candidate, George McGovern, whose platform was for an immediate end to the war. The war, as it turned out, was ending anyway. Without fanfare, the last American combat forces left Vietnam before the end of November 1972. Only about 16,000 Army advisors were left in the country, ironically the same number Kennedy had sent to Vietnam when he opted to escalate the American involvement in 1963.

A confident post-election Nixon sent a letter to South Vietnamese President Thieu trying to reassure him that the United States would "take swift and severe retaliatory action" if North Vietnam violated the proposed peace treaty, which Nixon hoped would be finalized soon in Paris. Thieu had grave doubts about the treaty and had to be browbeaten into accepting its necessity. Kissinger returned to Paris wrap up the agreement and was surprised when Le Duc Tho refused to negotiate further. That was Hanoi's mistake.

Nixon ordered Operation Linebacker II, a maximum effort of U.S. bombing against Hanoi and Haiphong, to be unleashed unless the Communists returned to the negotiating table within seventy-two hours. When Hanoi did not respond, the most intensive bombing campaign of the entire war began. Wave after wave of B-52s pounded military targets in North Vietnam, dropping more than 100,000 bombs over a course of eleven days. Twelve hundred surface-to-air missiles were fired at American aircraft, downing twenty-six aircraft, fifteen of them B-52s.

The 1972 Christmas bombing

The *Washington Post* described the 1972 Christmas bombing of Hanoi (Linebacker II) as "the most savage and senseless act of war ever visited, over a scant ten days, by one sovereign people over another."[33] The *New York Times,* the *Washington Post, Time, Newsweek,* CBS, and other mainstream media outlets reported that the bombing was indiscriminate, that its purpose was to cause heavy civilian casualties, that it would stiffen Hanoi's resolve, that it would cause serious losses of United States aircraft and manpower, and that it would shame the United States in its own eyes and in the eyes of the world.

They couldn't have been more wrong if they had tried. Which they had.

The bombing was *not* indiscriminate—*no* bombing using American planes ever was. Civilians were *not* targeted; in fact, pains were taken to avoid civilian casualties. There were 754 B-52 sorties and 640 fighter-bomber sorties dropping 20,000 tons of bombs from 18 to 29 December

1972. By the North Vietnamese account, 1,318[34] civilians were killed in the bombing. Or to put it another way, during the bombing of Hamburg, Germany, in 1944, half the tonnage of bombs killed nearly 20 times as many people. Again, the bombing was not to inflict undue suffering on North Vietnamese civilians, but to demonstrate Nixon's resolution and the awesome power of American air forces.

The Christmas bombing did *not* stiffen North Vietnam's resolve. On the contrary, it finally forced North Vietnam to capitulate at the Paris peace talks. On December 15, 1972, Nixon had sent a note to Hanoi demanding that the Communist government return to the negotiating table within seventy-two hours or face the consequences. The North Vietnamese ignored him—until the bombing. On December 26, Hanoi indicated it would resume negotiations. Nixon halted the bombing on December 28. On January 8, 1973, Kissinger and the North Vietnamese met in Paris. On January 13, a basic agreement was hammered out, which was ratified on January 23, 1973.

The United States did *not* incur disproportionate, unsustainable losses in the bombing. Twenty-six aircraft were lost, forty-three Americans were killed, and forty-nine were captured. These were hard losses—as all losses in war are. But these American pilots and crews had destroyed North Vietnam's air fields, exhausted the enemy's supply of surface to air missiles (during the last three days of the bombing, United States aircraft were virtually unfired upon), and almost obliterated North Vietnam's railroads, petrol

Watch Out for That Tree!

Carpet bombing has often been cited as one of the many "crimes against humanity" the Americans were guilty of. "Crimes against jungles" doesn't have the same ring. Not a single city in the North or South was "carpet bombed" during the war. Hanoi, Haiphong, and all the other cities were not smoldering heaps of ash during or after the war. (Smoldering heaps of ashes being what carpet bombed cities look like.)

dumps, and electrical grid. From the perspective of risk and reward, gain and loss, the Christmas bombing might have been the most successful campaign carried out in the war.

Of course, thanks to the American media, the bombing did create outrage among the anti-war left in the United States and Europe. But the Christmas bombing was the most *misreported* story of the Vietnam War since the Tet Offensive. You didn't need to read *Pravda* to get the Communist propaganda spin—you could read the *New York Times*. American liberal politicians were outraged. The major-media were apoplectic. Phrases along the lines of "the most vicious attack in military history" and "the work of a madman" and "a crime against humanity" were tossed about like confetti by pundits and politicians around the world. Kissinger was compared to Himmler; Nixon was burned in effigy; protest

Bombing Swords into Ploughshares

In a letter to the editor of the *New York Times* (May 1, 1975) responding to a review of his book *The Prestige Press and the Christmas Bombing, 1972*, Martin F. Herz wrote, "The Pentagon (in April 1973) offered photographic proof that Hanoi, whose wanton 'destruction' by 'carpet bombing' had been protested by the *New York Times* and *Washington Post*, was virtually intact after the bombing and that—with relatively minor exceptions—only military targets had been hit. The *Times* had the good grace to report this on its front page a month afterward; the other prestige media buried the news or spiked it altogether. Far from being wanton and cruel, the Christmas bombing of 1972 speeded up the armistice."[35]

marches rocked the streets.[36] And, by the way, the bombing accomplished exactly what it was intended to do. Another point the pundits seemed to have missed.

Endgame

It's a miracle that the United States and South Vietnam achieved *anything* by talking to the North Vietnamese in Paris—and not just because of the theatre of the absurd intransigence of the North Vietnamese. The talks were held against the background noise of the United States Congress, the liberal media, and the anti-war activists calling for the United States to get out of Vietnam at *any* price. The American negotiators had the leverage of what our troops achieved in the field, but the North Vietnamese had the leverage of the Western "peace movement," which led them to believe that there would be no long-term American commitment to South Vietnam.

At the end, the major sticking point of the Peace Agreement was the section that allowed North Vietnamese troops to remain in South Vietnam after the ceasefire. The South Vietnamese finally accepted this with the proviso that the United States would never allow the North Vietnamese to resupply or replace the troops with massive border crossings. At the time of the signing of the Peace Agreement, the South Vietnamese Army, with American armament and training, was more than capable of dealing with the North Vietnamese units that were left in South Vietnam. Of course, the North Vietnamese broke the agreement as soon as they had recovered sufficiently from the pounding the United States military had given them for eight years, and the United States Congress broke our promise to prevent that (over the anguished protests of President Gerald Ford). The North Vietnamese viewed the Peace Agreement from the start as a way to allow them to rebuild and rearm without American harassment. They had no intention of living up to the agreement, whatever its final terms.

The Paris Peace Accords were signed by the United States, North Vietnam, South Vietnam, and the Viet Cong. The United States agreed to withdraw its remaining forces within sixty days and Hanoi agreed to release all American POWs during the same period. One hundred fifty thousand NVA troops were still within South Vietnam. Any offensive activity by them would be a violation of the agreement—though what else these troops were doing in South Vietnam other than waiting for an opportunity to violate the agreement was an open question. President Thieu thought he knew the unfortunate answer. That was the bad news. So, too, was the fact that two South Vietnamese governments were recognized, Thieu's government and the Viet Cong, with the hope that there would be a government of national reconciliation.

The good news was that South Vietnam was still a country, an independent, sovereign state that had withstood everything the Communists could throw at it. The Nixon-Kissinger plan for ending the war had succeeded. What was necessary to ensure its continued success was America's commitment to defend the treaty and punish Communist violations of it. Hanoi had learned that it needed to respect Nixon's tenacity, and China—with whom North Vietnam was barely on speaking terms—was seemingly enamored with the old anti-Communist from San Clemente, regarding him as a great world statesman worthy of its respect. Nixon trusted not only to force and diplomacy, though; he also offered the Hanoi government aid to help rebuild North Vietnam.

More good news: America's troops were home. The South Vietnamese were at (a tenuous) peace for the first time in a generation. Kissinger and Le Duc Tho shared the 1973 Nobel Peace Prize (though Tho refused to accept his. Hanoi was in no mood to celebrate; it had other ambitions).

In the United States, the only significant public celebration of the end of the America's involvement in the Vietnam War took place in February 1973 with the arrival of the 591 American POWs, mostly airmen, from North Vietnam's prisons. America rejoiced at the sight of the men returning to their families and friends. Some of these POWs had survived seven years of torture and brutal, sub-human conditions. Almost to a man, the POWs thanked President Nixon for getting them out of North Vietnam. Initially, there was a concerted, diplomatic effort to play down the fact that the POWs had been tortured and criminally abused, in order to advance the peace with North Vietnam. But as the POWs' personal stories trickled out over the coming years, America was incensed at Hanoi's cruelty and thrilled by the dignity and strength with which the POWs had endured. They never gave up. After long years of a divisive, bitter conflict, America wanted heroes, and it found them in the men who had been prisoners.

Over the course of the war, nearly three million Americans had served in the theater, with an estimated 500,000 seeing actual combat. There were 47,244 killed in combat including 8,000 pilots. Non-combat deaths accounted for another 11,000 and 153,329 were seriously injured. More than 2,400 POWs/MIAs were unaccounted for at war's end.[37] It is obscene to say these sacrifices were in vain. It is without reason to say that America's servicemen "lost" anything. The South Vietnamese were not living under Communist rule. They had a window of opportunity, with American air cover, to build and train their army and air force while North Vietnam

Presidents of South Vietnam, 1955–1975: A Rough Two Decades

Ngo Dinh Diem, 1955–1963

Duong Van Minh, 1963–1964

Nguyen Khanh, January to February 1964

Duong Van Minh, February to March 1964

Nguyen Khanh, March to August 1964

Provisional Leadership Committee, August to September 1964

Duong Van Minh, September to October 1964

Phan Khac Suu, 1964–1965

Nguyen Van Thieu, 1965–1975

Tran Van Huong, 1975

Duong Van Minh, 1975

was licking its substantial wounds. Thailand and the rest of non-Communist Southeast Asia could continue the substantial economic growth that was just beginning to germinate.

While it is true that Nixon had to settle for less than a perfect peace treaty, it isn't true that it had no chance of succeeding. Many of the arguments against the plan were spurious, such as we didn't have enough B-52s to continue bombing Hanoi because we lost fifteen in the 1972 Christmas bombing. (While we had lost fifteen bombers, North Vietnam had lost all its surface-to-air missiles; an arms race against North Vietnam and its Soviet suppliers was one we could win.)

What effectively terminated the Paris peace accords was the unraveling Watergate scandal. It emboldened an already hostile Congress to pass—by a veto-proof 278 to 124 vote in the House and 64 to 26 vote in the Senate—the Case-Church Amendment to the Defense Appropriations bill. It prohibited any further America military involvement in Southeast Asia, effective August 15, 1973. Liberal Democrats in Congress had hounded Nixon to reach a peace agreement in Vietnam. He had. Then these very same Democrats effectively undid the agreement by voiding our guarantees to President Thieu.

In July 1973, the U.S. Navy removed its mines blocking North Vietnamese ports, living up to American obligations under the peace settlement—the result was a massive influx of Soviet materiel for the NVA, which was champing at the bit for another invasion of South Vietnam now that Uncle Sam was out of the picture. And he wasn't likely to come back. Not only had Congress passed the Case-Church Amendment, but in November 1973, over Nixon's veto, Congress enacted the War Powers Resolution. It required that the president obtain congressional support within ninety days of sending American troops abroad for military action. The North Vietnamese knew that no such support would be forthcoming.

On August 9, 1974, President Nixon resigned rather than face impeachment. Gerald Ford, a decent man but in a weak position, was sworn in as the 38th U.S. president. In October, the North Vietnamese Politburo met and made the decision to launch an invasion of South Vietnam in 1975.

The North Vietnamese were well aware that Congress had no interest in reengaging in Indochina, and saw how Congress was begrudgingly appropriating minimal military aid to South Vietnam. In December, the North Vietnamese attacked Phouc Long in South Vietnam—apparently to see what reaction it might get from the United States. The answer: strong words from President Ford, but no military action.

Thanks a lot, guys

On February 21, 1970, the first of the "secret negotiations" between North Vietnam and U.S. representatives was held in Paris. Le Duc Tho, future Noble Peace Prize decliner, told Kissinger that he had "seen many statements by the Senate Foreign Relations Committee, by the Democratic Party, by Mr. [Clark] Clifford [former secretary of defense under LBJ], which have demanded the total withdrawal of American forces, the change of Thieu-Ky-Khiem [the government of South Vietnam], and the appointment of a successor to Ambassador Lodge."[38]

A lot of time and trouble could have been saved if the U.S. Democrats and the liberal media had simply teamed up with North Vietnam so that Nixon and Kissinger could have just negotiated with them all at the same time.

The serious reality is that the anti-war crowd in Congress, the media, and academia were demanding a settlement to the war while they were doing nearly everything possible to make sure that no reasonable (save abandoning the South Vietnamese) settlement was possible.

North Vietnam had the fifth largest army in the world, and a Soviet military supplier that was unstinting in its generosity. Hanoi began sharpening bayonets. Secretary of Defense James Schlesinger testified that Congress was preventing the United States from fulfilling its promises to President Thieu of "severe retaliatory action" if North Vietnam violated the Paris peace treaty.[40] Such violations were happening, and Congress would not let the United States government respond. The next week, January 21, 1975, President Gerald Ford stated the obvious: the United States was unwilling to re-enter the Vietnam War.

Fifty-five days after the NVA launched their attack, Saigon fell, April 30, 1975. A red and blue Viet Cong flag flew over the presidential palace. South Vietnam's last president, Duong van "Big" Minh (an oversized, in Vietnamese terms, general who had been president on three previous occasions, dating back to 1963), broadcast a message of unconditional surrender. Millions of Americans including former combatants choked up in anger and disgust.

There will never be a definitive answer to the question of who "won" in Vietnam. It was never America's goal—and this was perhaps its folly—to "defeat" North Vietnam. The United States fought a limited war with limited goals, and when our troops were withdrawn it was with those goals apparently achieved—an independent South Vietnam and the containment of Communist aggression so that it didn't spread throughout Southeast Asia. The United States paid a steep price, but those names on the wall of the Vietnam veterans memorial in Washington, D.C., represent a free Thailand, a semi-capitalist China, a partially capitalist (lest it

Treaty? We Don't Have No Stinkin' Treaty!

"In the first two months after the 1973 cease-fire, more than 30,000 North Vietnamese soldiers were infiltrated into South Vietnam via Laos and Cambodia.... During 1973, the North Vietnamese constructed 12 airfields in the South [and] installed SAM-2 missiles at Khe Sanh."[39]

starve) Vietnam whose people are (to the chagrin of the government) over-whelmingly pro-American, and a Southeast Asia far more stable than it

Patriots, Trouble-makers, or Just Liars

President Truman (1949): "… All nations and all peoples are free to gov-ern themselves as they see fit. The United States would 'strengthen freedom-loving nations against the dangers of aggression.'"

President Eisenhower (1953): "Conceiving the defense of freedom, like freedom itself, to be one and indivisible, we hold all continents and peoples in equal regard and honor."

President Kennedy (1961): "Let every nation know, whether it wishes us well or ill, that we shall pay any price, bear any burden, meet any hard-ship, support any friend, oppose any foe to assure the survival and suc-cess of liberty."

President Johnson (1965): "Terrific dangers and troubles that we once called 'foreign' now constantly live among us. If American lives must end, and American treasure be spilled, in countries that we barely know, then it is the price that change has demanded of conviction and of our enduring covenant."

President Nixon (1969): "I'm going to bomb those bastards like they've never been bombed before." (Kissinger)

"For a great power to abandon a small country to tyranny simply to obtain a respite from our own travail seemed to me—and still seems to me—profoundly immoral and destructive of our efforts to build a new and ultimately more peaceful pattern of international relations."[44]

U.S. Congress (1973–1975): Aw, to hell with it.

likely would have been had Hanoi triumphantly marched through Saigon in the 1960s. There is no doubt, of course, that South Vietnam, Laos, and Cambodia lost the war. North Vietnam's victory brought them incredible suffering. It is not clear, however, what North Vietnam won after our departure. Yes, the Communists unified the country under their tyranny and became a regional military power that went on to fight China and Cambodia. But while the Communist regime remains in place, it defends an obviously bankrupt ideology—and the death toll it not only inflicted, but endured (more than 1.1 million men lost) to impose that cruel, oppressive, and falsified ideology is one that no Christian westerner, certainly, could justify.

What must haunt the dreams of South Vietnamese refugees is what could have been. The collapse of South Vietnam was not inevitable. Former South Vietnamese ambassador Bui Diem describes in his book, *The Jaws of History*, how during the final Communist push into his country, "the entire North Vietnamese force, with its enormous quantities of Soviet and Chinese equipment, was spread out in the open, advancing in long columns along the major highways, more vulnerable to air attack than at any time during the war. At Xuan Loc, on Saigon's outer defensive perimeter, South Vietnam's Eighteenth Division was throwing back every assault their enemies launched at them. Intervention by American air power alone, the kind of intervention Nixon and Kissinger has so fervently promised in 1973, could have destroyed the exposed columns, crippling the Communist's war-making capacity for years. A resupplied and re-encouraged South Vietnamese army might then have taken back a great deal of what was lost."[41] Every major battle fought by the ARVN and the United States against the North Vietnamese army supports this view. But America was now the "helpless giant" of Nixon's nightmares, a hapless Gulliver tied down by bonds imposed by a Lilliputian Democrat Congress, the radical left, and the major media. Because of those Lilliputians, some twenty million South Vietnamese, their children, and their children beyond them were sacrificed to Communism.

Chapter Five

THE ANTI-WAR MOVEMENT

From 1965 to 1973, if anything received more press than the War in Vietnam, it was the Anti-War Movement. In the public mind, the anti-war movement could be rolled into that violent juggernaut of social unrest that seemed to tear at America's seams—racial strife, hippies, demonstrations, riots, drugs, the sexual revolution, the Black Panthers—they all seemed to come together at some point. If confronted with a long-haired, crazed-eyed individual, you didn't know whether you were facing a tirade about the war, a sales pitch for drugs, an impassioned screed about the evil U.S. government, or perhaps a mugging by someone whose mind had been eaten away by LSD or heroin while he was enjoying a draft deferment in college and perpetual graduate school to maintain his draft-ineligible status.

Here's an unpalatable truth from someone who fought in Vietnam. It struck me at the time—and even more so after studying the anti-war movement—that many people in the anti-war movement preferred the excitement of protesting to attending class (if they were students), or the hallucinogenic or earthy pleasures of hanging out with the free drugs and free sex folks, or were driven, as people often are, by fashion: it was easy and fashionable and fun and a great way to flatter yourself and your moral superiority over your parents and "the establishment" and "the squares" to be against the war; it took some moral fortitude, and plain old

Guess what?

‡ The so-called "peace movement" was riddled with Communist sympathizers and others who unknowingly spouted Communist propaganda

‡ Many members of the Vietnam Veterans Against the War (VVAW) never actually fought in Vietnam

‡ Communism, which America fought against in Vietnam, was by far the bloodiest ideology the world has ever known

A Book the Viet Cong (and Vietnam Veterans Against the War) Wouldn't Want You to Read

Stolen Valor, B. G. Burkett and Glenna Whitley (Verity Press, 1998).

physical courage, to be for it and to put on that uniform and head out to defend the people of South Vietnam.

If you strip out the authentic radicals and Communists (the minority vanguard of the movement) and the fashionable "peace activists" looking for a good time while inflating their egos, is anyone left? Well, sure. Not a great many, but there were of course serious protestors who knew something about the issues involved, loved and admired America, and wanted peace for the world. One of them lives in Maine and runs a wood-carving shop and the other married money and lives in Boca Raton.

What suggests that the anti-war crowd wasn't serious about their mission?

Well, maybe the way they defined "peace." Peace was what the United States was trying to defend—the peace that was supposed to exist between the sovereign nations of North Vietnam and South Vietnam, that was supposed to exist between North Vietnam and Laos, that was supposed to exist between North Vietnam and Cambodia. It was the Communists who were the aggressors throughout Southeast Asia. It was they who denied the right of non-Communist nations within their reach to exist. The peace they offered was a peace of submission to the most oppressive and totalitarian political system the world has ever known. The peace the American military sought to create was a peace between sovereign nations—a containment of aggressive international Communism so that free institutions could develop outside of its orbit.

This might seem plain as day, but the anti-war activists never seemed to grasp it. One particularly useful American idiot, Jane Fonda, ranted on Radio Hanoi that the North Vietnamese were only fighting for their independence. From whom, one might ask. The French were long gone.

Maybe the anti-war crowd was driven by a heart-felt opposition to this war or any war, maybe they were pacifists. But if so, why were so many so sympathetic to the non-pacifistic Viet Cong? In any event, the majority of all American troops in Vietnam were volunteers, so those bleeding hearts with college deferments didn't have to go, and could enjoy the sexual revolution at home rather than risk getting their manhood shot off in a rice paddy. Between two-thirds and three-fourths of all combatants, and those killed in action, were volunteers. (The discrepancy between the numbers is that some unknown number of men volunteered to escape the draft, so were not truly, strictly speaking, volunteers.)

True, you might oppose the war because South Vietnam (according to the *New York Times* et al) didn't treat its own citizens very well. Of course, the alternative to South Vietnam's government was Hanoi's, which eliminated its class enemies with bullets (if you were lucky).

True, you might be anti-war because a regime that drove Buddhists to self-immolation had to be pretty unsavory. Of course, the Hanoi alternative was an atheistic regime that snuffed religion out entirely.

True, you might be anti-war because South Vietnam's regime had a reputation for corruption and cronyism. Of course, the alternative was Hanoi's one-party state.

Do We Really Need to Spell This Out for You?

Many of the useful idiots who visited North Vietnam during the war commented on the lack of demonstrations against the government in Hanoi, taking this as a sign of the great popularity of the Communist regime.

South Korea was not a model state when we defended it during the Korean War. But it is certainly a relatively stable, prosperous, democratic state now, and a world removed in terms of its freedom from its Communist neighbor to the north.

The truth was that remove the Communist threat—and the terrorism and war that the Communists brought—and South Vietnam was a peaceful, family-oriented, hard-working, physically beautiful, nice place to live. Its government was far from perfect, but neither is Mexico's, nor our own.

Some might have opposed the war because they were isolationists. But America's bipartisan, postwar consensus was that we had a responsibility to contain Communist aggression. In any event, the anti-war protesters liked to assume they represented a higher morality, and it would be

Ho, Ho, Ho Chi Minh, Mao and Che Are Going to Win

According to most estimates, Chairman Mao bests Stalin who bests Hitler in the sweepstakes for the biggest mass murderer in history. Yet, he remains for a disconcerting number of people on the Left some sort of hero, an ideological guiding light cited by no less than two early appointees in the Obama administration, Van Jones and Anita Dunn. Mao was by any measure a monster, presiding over mass executions, reeducation camps, and the imposition of a totalitarian society. His personal habits and attitudes were as bizarre as they were heinous. He once suggested to Kissinger that China export millions of Chinese women to the United States. China, he explained, had an excess of women that were a burden on the country. His predilection for sleeping with young girls (as young as eleven years old) came from his belief that sleeping with virgins would invigorate an old man. Much like those who wear "Che" tee-shirts—with the image of Che Guevara, who ran Cuba's political prisons and took a personal (not to mention sadistic) interest in executions—the wearing of Mao shirts (particularly by women) exhibits an abysmal disregard for morality and history.

I Heard It through the Communist Grapevine

Communist bloc intelligence services worked overtime cranking out false tales of American war crimes in Vietnam. Inevitably, these were recounted as truth by people who should have known better. Ion Mihai Pacepa, the highest ranking intelligence officer ever to defect from the Soviet bloc, noted that "As a spy chief and a general in the former Soviet satellite of Romania, I produced the very same [anti-war] vitriol [anti-war veteran and future senator and presidential candidate John] Kerry repeated to the U.S. Congress almost word for word and planted it in leftist movements throughout Europe. KGB Chairman Yuri Andropov managed our anti-Vietnam War operation. He often bragged about having damaged the U.S. foreign-policy consensus, poisoned the domestic debate in the U.S., and built a credibility gap between America and European public opinion through our disinformation operations. Vietnam was, he once told me, our most significant success."[1]

hard to square isolationism with idealism. At best, one might call it naïve; at worst, short-sighted and selfish.

What about the idea that Vietnam was a "proxy" war, with the United States on one side and the Soviet Union and Red China on the other? To the Communists, all states were, in a sense, proxy states meant to advance Communist ideology and revolution; Communism was an international movement—"workers of the world unite!"—and that was why China and Russia supplied millions and millions of tons of war equipment, tens of thousands of troops and support personnel, millions of tons of food, and billions of rubles and yen to the North Vietnamese. But the United States was not using South Vietnam as a "proxy." We were not there to strike at Red China or the Soviet Union or to advance democracy or free enterprise. We were there because South Vietnam had been attacked, and because defending it struck men like John F. Kennedy as the decent thing to do.

"Oh, come on, were the Commies really that bad?"

That, in a phrase, was the underlying assumption of much of the anti-war Left. It's a pretty awful assumption. The short answer is yes, they were that bad if you were a member of the clergy, or a landowner, or a capitalist, or wealthy, or valued freedom, or were opposed to inescapable state control and indoctrination, or if you wore glasses (a sign of deviationist intellectualism at various times in Cambodia or China), or became in any way an enemy of the Communist Party.

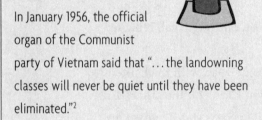

Well, That's One Solution

In January 1956, the official organ of the Communist party of Vietnam said that "…the landowning classes will never be quiet until they have been eliminated."[2]

Globally, Communism was the largest and most deadly social experiment known to mankind. When it collapsed in the 1990s, it had killed, according to the best estimates, 100,000,000 men, women, and children. More than 30,000,000 more were killed in its wars against other countries. This was the ideology of the North Vietnamese regime that was supported by the movie stars, college students, professional agitators, academics, and leftist journalists who prided themselves on being anti-war.

And they weren't the only ones. Most people assume that it was the young in the 1960s and 1970s who were most opposed to the war. That's because most media coverage was of student protests. But actually, statistically speaking, if you were opposed to the war, you were an "old woman." Polls taken throughout the war were consistent—older people were more opposed to the war than younger people, and women more than men.

In a series of twenty-two polls taken from May 1965 through May 1971, support for the war was greater among those under thirty than those over forty-nine. In fact, the support for the war was greater from those under thirty than those between the ages of thirty and forty-nine in all of the polls except September 1966 and September 1969.

As late as February 1968, the majority of Americans were definite hawks. Twenty-five percent wanted to "gradually broaden and intensify our military operations," and another 28 percent wanted to "start an all-out crash effort in the hope of winning the war quickly even at the risk of China or Russia entering the war." If the polls are to be believed, support for the war declined after 1968 (hardly surprising after the defeatist blather of the media after TeT). But the most important polls to remember are the presidential elections. The American people elected Richard Nixon in 1968 and reelected him in a landslide in 1972.

Why Is That?

Somehow "ex-Communist," or even "sympathetic to Communists" isn't the resume killer that "ex-Nazi" is.

"Jane, you ignorant slut." (Actually Dan Aykroyd to Jane Curtin on Saturday Night Live, but...)

So who *were* the visible and angry protesters?

Surely the most visible would be actress and political activist Jane Fonda. Her actions during the Vietnam War defined her for most Americans. For those few who don't know—she supported the enemy. There really is no other way to put it. She traveled to Hanoi, called American soldiers "war criminals," thanked the Russians for supporting the North Vietnamese, posed for photos sitting in a North Vietnamese anti-aircraft battery, and dismissed American POWs as liars when they said they had been tortured.

Jane Fonda bought the whole anti-war program down to accepting Communism as not such a bad thing after all. Or, as she put it in a speech to Duke University students in 1970, "If you understood what Communism was, you would hope and pray on your knees that we would some-day become Communist."[3]

Fonda's understanding of the war always seemed a bit sketchy, though this did not inhibit her in the slightest in leading protests against it. During her tour of North Vietnam she said, "Every man, woman and child in this country has a determination like a bright flame, buoying them, strengthening their determination to go forward, to fight for freedom and independence." Fonda was perhaps unaware that North Vietnam *was* independent; it was trying to deny South Vietnam's independence. And freedom? Well, Jane thought the North Vietnamese had a better idea about that than we did. "And what interests me so much is that as an American...the one unifying quality I believe about the American people, the common denominator that we all share, is the love for freedom and democracy. The problem is that definition of freedom and democracy has been distorted for us, and we have to redefine what that means. But the Vietnamese who have been fighting for four thousand years know very well."[4] Tell it to the boat people, Jane.

Only in America could a woman like this be made a gazillionaire through aerobics videos and Hollywood stardom. Jane Fonda pandered pathetically to the Communists; she used her celebrity to flatter anti-war activists; and anti-war leaders flattered her by feigning to take her seriously.

Not the VFW

In many ways the most harmful anti-war activists, and the most despicable, were the Vietnam Veterans Against the War (VVAW). Many of these "veterans" were exposed as frauds or charlatans, with no service at all in Vietnam, and their claims of committing war crimes in Vietnam were immoral, dishonest, and the product of sometimes tormented imaginations. The VVAW was a "veterans" group supported by Jane Fonda—need more be said?

In case it does, we can note that the VVAW was a radical group founded in 1967. It reached its apotheosis in January 1971 when it held its Winter Soldier Investigation in Detroit. The "investigation" was largely funded by Jane Fonda and Mark Lane, a JFK assassination conspiracy theorist who had already published a book blaming Americans for war crimes in Vietnam—a book which had already been discredited by Neil Sheehan in *The New York Times Book Review*, where he established that the book was full of demonstrably false stories by men who had never actually served in Vietnam; the Winter Soldier Investigation would produce more of the same. Also supporting the "investigation" were Dick Gregory, Phil Ochs, Graham Nash, David Crosby, and Donald Sutherland. It was an "event," and it promoted the idea that American servicemen in Vietnam were guilty of wholesale rape, murder, and other criminal behavior. In that cause, truth or accuracy was irrelevant. As the scholar Guenter Lewy noted in his classic book *America in Vietnam*, "The VVAW's use of fake witnesses and the failure to cooperate with military authorities [who were willing to investigate the allegations made at the Winter Soldier Investigation] and to provide crucial details of the incidents casts serious doubt on the professed desire to serve the causes of justice and humanity. It is more likely that this inquiry, like others earlier and later, had primarily political motives and goals."[5] That's a polite and academic way of saying what B. G. Burkett and Glenna Whitley concluded in the investigation of the Winter Soldier Investigation—it was "a classic example of turning reality on its head."[6] Which is a polite way of saying what actual veterans say: "It was a load of crap."

But it brought notoriety to VVAW member John Kerry, who was invited to testify before the Senate Foreign Relations Committee on April 22, 1971. Anti-war senators, especially in the wake of the My Lai massacre, were happy to use any available tool to discredit the war, even if it meant throwing slime over the reputations of the brave and honorable men whom the

What Is It about Liberals and the Truth?

The VVAW did not manage to attract *all* the combat wannabees. In the 1992 Democratic presidential primaries, Senator Tom Harkin of Iowa claimed that he had served a year as a combat and reconnaissance pilot in Vietnam. Okay, not actually in Vietnam, but combat missions over Cuba. Did I say Cuba? I meant ferrying missions out of Atsugi, Japan. (I always get Japan and Cuba mixed up. They're both islands aren't they?) But he did ferry aircraft into Vietnam, twelve times. Okay, he was a Vietnam *era* vet. And he knows how to fly. And he was stationed in Cuba.[8] Of course he was in good company. In the 2000 U.S. census, over 12 million people claimed to be veterans of the Vietnam War.[9] Fewer than 3 million served.

After the Winter Soldier Investigations, attended by some veterans who didn't even know they had attended until they saw their names used, the VVAW's big event was when a gaggle of veterans, real or alleged, threw their war medals over a fence in front of the Capitol building. Most prominent of the flingers was John Kerry. Years later, after his election to the Senate, John Kerry displayed his medals on the wall of his Capitol Hill office. When asked, Kerry admitted the medals he had thrown were not his own. Just another fraud perpetrated by the VVAW.

United States government had called to duty and sent into battle. Kerry told the senators that the Winter Soldier Investigation had found more than 150 Vietnam Vets who "testified to war crimes committed in Southeast Asia, not isolated incidents but crimes committed on a day-to-day basis with full awareness of officers at all levels of command.... They told the stories at times they had personally raped, cut off ears, cut off heads, taped wires from portable telephones to human genitals and turned up the power, cut off limbs, blown up bodies, randomly shot at civilians, razed villages in a fashion reminiscent of Genghis Khan, shot cattle and dogs for fun, poisoned stocks, and generally ravaged the countryside of South Vietnam in addition to the normal ravage of war...." Questioned by the committee following his remarks, Kerry claimed that 200,000 Vietnamese a year had been "murdered by the United States of America."[7] A quick tabulation would result in Kerry's claim meaning that the U.S. had "murdered" over a million of our ally's citizens by the time he testified. And we took this guy seriously?

Campfire Tales for Radicals

Later Army Criminal Investigation Division (CID) investigations of the charges made by the VVAW/Winter Soldier Investigation proved fruitless, as they could find no one willing to testify or document statements and claims made at the Winter Soldier Investigation.

What substantiation did Kerry have for these outrageous claims? The answer was—next to nothing that could withstand serious scrutiny. In fact, as soon as these stories began to be investigated, they started to fall apart. There were no documentation, proof, or sworn affidavits, and precious few details. Hardly surprising, those "veterans" who claimed they themselves had committed serious war crimes disappeared. The U.S. prosecutes even minor war crimes (over two hundred during the war), unlike the Communists who promote them.

A True Atrocity

The My Lai Massacre—the horrific killing of approximately 350 civilians, including old men, women, and children—was an act of insanity that became notorious precisely because of its uniqueness, as a violation of American ideas of morality and decency. It was the only atrocity of that scale ever substantiated by documentation.

There is no doubt that war crimes and reprehensible behavior occurred in Vietnam. There is no doubt that commanders sometimes tried to cover up criminal actions to avoid scandal. There is also no doubt that such things happen in every war, even the most pristinely fought. There is no excuse for such actions. However, we should judge the long, brutal, and frustrating war in Vietnam as a war like all others. While evil can never be banished from the human heart and mistakes can never be banished from human behavior, such outrages were rare on the American side. They were not rare—they were policy—on the Communist side. Ignoring that fact only highlights the ignorance and bias of the anti-war movement.

Six great myths of the anti-war movement

If war is horrendous—and it unmistakably is—is pacifism noble? The nineteenth-century British philosopher, economist, and political commentator John Stuart Mill probably answered the question best.

"War is an ugly thing, but not the ugliest of things. The decayed and degraded state of moral and patriotic feeling which thinks that nothing is worth war is much worse. The person who has nothing for which he is willing to fight, nothing which is more important than his own personal safety, is a miserable creature and has no chance of being free unless made and kept so by the exertions of better men than himself."[11]

The anti-war Left dealt more in protests than in argument; but when they did make an argument, they usually focused on one of six basic themes—all of which were wrong.

"The government of South Vietnam is corrupt and unworthy of our support"

Well, the United States Congress is sometimes corrupt and unworthy of our support, too. The real question is: As opposed to what? South Vietnam might not have been a model liberal democracy, but it was worlds removed from the murderous Communist totalitarianism of North Vietnam. Whatever its flaws, if you lived in South Vietnam, you were largely

A Good Man Gone Wrong

The fever swamp irrationality of the anti-war movement was highly contagious, infecting not just college students, senators, and Hollywood types, but men you might have hoped would have known better, men like the Reverend Martin Luther King, Jr.

King's April 1967 "Declaration on the War in Vietnam" called Ngo Dinh Diem "one of the most vicious modern dictators" (better check those statistics again), claimed that only a quarter of the Viet Cong were Communists (even the Viet Cong would have taken umbrage at that; if they weren't Communists they were just murdering bandits—though of course they were that, too), and said the United States had "no honorable intentions in Vietnam. It will become clear that our minimal expectation is to occupy it as an American colony, and men will not refrain from thinking that our maximum hope is to goad China into a war so that we may bomb their nuclear installations."[10] He made plenty of other obviously false accusations in the speech as well. In fact, as some noted at the time, the speech could have been lifted practically word for word from Communist propaganda. King was not a Communist, but too many liberals in those days were willing to accept Communists as only slightly misguided liberals.

free to work, worship, travel, and live how and where you wanted—unlike your neighbors in the North. The United States government believed it had a compelling national interest to contain the spread of Communism, and it made a political and moral commitment to keeping South Vietnam free from the invading North Vietnamese Communists.

"The Vietnam War is a civil war that needs to be decided by its own people"

People who trotted out this argument usually tried to downplay the involvement of the North Vietnamese—something that seems transparently laughable now.

Still, it is true that early terrorist attacks in the villages and cities of South Vietnam were mostly carried out by *local* Viet Cong. Many of these terrorists were former Viet Minh soldiers who remained in South Vietnam after the 1954 Geneva Accords dividing North and South Vietnam. The war of terror the Viet Cong waged against the civil government of South Vietnam was, in proportion to the United States population, the equivalent of assassinating tens of thousands of American mayors and city councilmen—and all this done at the direction of, and with the direct support of, a foreign government. By 1959, the North was sending its own regular troops into South Vietnam, and in 1960 publicly announced its intention to overthrow the South Vietnamese government (something Hanoi had already resolved to do after the Geneva Accords). The plain fact is that from the mid-1960s until its ultimate defeat in 1975, South Vietnam was fighting an invading army. Pat Nixon said it best: "Jane Fonda should have been in Hanoi asking them to stop their aggression, then there wouldn't be any conflict."[12]

The very fact that it took two decades and the loss of several million Vietnamese lives should prove that unification under the North Vietnamese Communist government was a far from universally desired goal. The Vietnam War was not a civil war among the people of South Vietnam; it was a war of Communist aggression by North Vietnam against the sovereign, free, internationally recognized nations of South Vietnam, Laos, and Cambodia.

"The American people don't support the war"

In a democracy, everyone wants to be in the majority, and poll after poll—not to mention the presidential landslide election of 1972—made it clear that the overwhelming majority of the American people supported Nixon's policy of "peace with honor" and opposed the anti-war Left. A Harris poll in 1969 showed that fewer than 10 percent of Americans wanted to pull out of South Vietnam if it meant a Communist victory.[13]

The liberal American journalists, academics, and politicians who turned against the war assumed that the American people shared their opinions. They didn't. Nor were the American people impressed by the draft-card burners and violent "pacifists" of the radical Left.

The vast majority of Americans (Richard Nixon's "silent majority") backed the war effort and stayed loyal to the "bear any burden, pay any price" vision of John F. Kennedy long after Kennedy's fellow liberals had abandoned it. Even today, 80 percent of Vietnam veterans say they would go back and do it all over again, even knowing the outcome, if their country called.[14]

"The Vietnam war is a proxy war between the capitalist West and the Communist East"

Even if the United States had not committed combat troops to defend South Vietnam from the North, even if South Vietnam had received no military aid from the United States, and even if North Vietnam had received no military aid from the Soviet Union and its satellites and Communist China, North and South Vietnam would still have been at war, because

Communist North Vietnam could not tolerate a non-Communist South Vietnam. The Communists backed the North's aggression, and we defended the South against it. The cause of the war was Ho Chi Minh's desire to carry the Communist revolution south (and, for that matter, west).

"The war is immoral"

This refuge of academics and left-leaning clergy only highlighted the shallow parochialism of the Left—as if, somehow, all was well with the world if we stayed out of it. But how is it immoral to defend a people from the terrorism and slavery (and murderous atheism) of Communism?

Of course, it can be difficult to argue the morality of any war—war *is* hell. But if we take the basic criteria of St. Augustine's guidelines for what constitutes a just war—that it be fought in a just cause (against Communist aggression would qualify), with a probability of success (we had successfully defended South Korea only a decade before), and bearing in mind proportional costs (better to live free, even at the cost of war, than submit to Communist tyranny makes sense to most of us)—we fought in a just cause.

In a draft (never delivered) memo to President Ford discussing the "lessons of Vietnam" Henry Kissinger wrote, "When we entered [the war], many did so in the name of morality. Before the war was over, many opposed it in the name of morality. But nobody spoke of the morality of consistency, or of the virtue of seeing something through...."[15] The real domestic immorality of the Vietnam War was the inconstancy of the liberals who got us into it.

"It's an unwinnable war"

There were many ways we could have won the Vietnam War, but we don't have to reiterate them, because we can point to how we did win, and how we could have preserved that victory: namely, through American airpower and the big guns of the U.S. Navy. They stopped the North Vietnamese Army every time they were allowed to do so.

The most striking example was the 1972 Easter Offensive launched by the North Vietnamese, the largest Communist offensive of the war. With almost all American troops out of the country, the ARVN repulsed attack after attack with the support of American air and naval forces. Of the 200,000 North Vietnamese attackers, nearly 100,000 were casualties, and North Vietnam's great gamble to pull off a stunning success ended in a miserable defeat.

The fact remains that after the 1973 Paris Peace Accords, all we had to do was provide air and naval support for our South Vietnamese ally. Far from being an unwinnable war, we had won. But after having achieved what the anti-war Left said couldn't be done, the liberal Democrat majority in Congress decided to prove them right after all by abrogating our commitments to South Vietnam. The argument that Vietnam was an unwinnable war was not true, but the Democrats in Congress decided to make it so.

Who made these arguments? The list is long. But you could include the likes of:

- Tom Hayden, the student radical turned California politico, most famous for helping organize the riots at the 1968 Democratic Convention in Chicago, and for being Mr. Jane Fonda.
- Daniel Ellsberg, the Vietnam veteran turned think tank analyst, who stole copies of the secret documents known

How Many Dominoes Have to Fall?

The Left sneers that the Domino Theory was a fallacy and has been discredited. They should try telling that to the people of Laos, Cambodia, and South Vietnam, whose countries fell—like dominoes—after the U.S. departed the region.

as the Pentagon Papers and gave them to the *New York Times.*

- Noam Chomsky, an academic whose specialty is linguistics (and freelance political radicalism), who liked to opine that the war "was basically an American attack on South Vietnam," that we were "fighting mostly unarmed people," and that the war was "the most obscene example of...[an] attempt by our country to impose its particular concept of order and stability throughout much of the world. By any objective standard, the United States has become the most aggressive power in the world, the greatest threat to peace, to national self-determination, and to international cooperation."[16]

- Abbie Hoffman, the egotistical and foul-mouthed (a combination common to many of the radicals) co-founder of the Youth International Party ("Yippies"), who was arrested (along with Tom Hayden) for organizing the riots at the 1968 Democratic National Convention; later busted for dealing cocaine, Hoffman went underground, emerging only for other random left-wing protests, and eventually committed suicide, apparently suffering from bipolar disorder.

- Jerry Rubin, another student radical who liked attention (he professed to admire the murderer Charles Manson), he was (like Hoffman and Hayden) arrested for organizing the riots at the 1968 Democratic National Convention; he later became a successful businessman (after he discovered that hucksterism could turn a profit).

- William Ramsey Clark, who moved from being LBJ's attorney general to joining the anti-war movement and offering his services as a defense attorney to a variety of anti-American figures, from Slobodan Milosevic to Saddam Hussein.

- The Reverend William Sloane Coffin, Jr., a left-wing clergyman willing to offer his blessing to a variety of "peace movements."

- Bill Ayers, the co-founder of the Weather Underground, a radical group opposed to the Vietnam War, he set off bombs at the U.S. Capitol, the Pentagon, and the New York City Police Department headquarters; an unreformed radical leftist, he is now a professor of education and helps design public school curricula; he regained national attention in 2008 when he was outed as an associate of Barack Obama. Once, while meeting with Vietnamese Communists (in Toronto, where the living is easier than in Hanoi) he received the gift of a ring made from an American aircraft shot down over North Vietnam. He said he was so moved by the gesture that he "left the room to cry." It made him realize that "America was an evil ... and that I was ... living inside the belly of the beast...."[17]

There were scores, if not hundreds, of anti-war activists who had their fifteen (or more) minutes of fame. Few amounted to anything more than being a foul nuisance. All, collectively, were harmful to the efforts to end the war and bring the troops safely home from Vietnam. And all were, in ways big and small, responsible for the loss of South Vietnam to the brutal rule and atrocities of the Communist North.

Chapter Six

COMING HOME

"We are honored to have had the opportunity to serve our country under difficult circumstances. We are profoundly grateful to our Commander in Chief and to our nation for this day. God Bless America."[1]

So spoke Navy Captain Jeremiah Denton, senior officer among the prisoners of war released by North Vietnam in February 1973, as he stepped out of the aircraft that delivered him to Clark Air Force Base in the Philippines. By the end of March, 589 other POWs had followed him home, ending the longest period of captivity for any group of American prisoners of war in American history.

Although the POWs returning from North Vietnam received a generous and well-deserved welcome, lesser known were those dozens of American soldiers and airmen who had been held captive in South Vietnam (by the Viet Cong), Cambodia, and Laos. In most cases their torture was less systematic, but their fight for existence in the jungles and mountains of Southeast Asia proved them no less heroic and resilient. One of them, an advisor to the South Vietnamese Marines, Captain Donald Cook, was the first Marine captured by the Viet Cong. Unlike the American aviators shot down over North Vietnam and interned at the infamous Hanoi Hilton, Marines and soldiers captured in the south were normally locked

Guess what?

‡ Vietnam Veterans are better off—financially, educationally, psychologically—than their peers who didn't serve

‡ The Army that served in Vietnam was the best educated, best trained, and most lethal to the enemy of any American army deployed to that time

‡ More than 80 percent of Vietnam veterans would serve again, even knowing the outcome

inside small bamboo cages in makeshift camps. These prisoners faced slow starvation, disease, and trying to survive in an extremely harsh environment. Captain Cook was awarded the Medal of Honor for his devotion to duty, his assistance to his fellow POWs, and his steadfast resistance to his Viet Cong captors.[2]

In the POW camps of North Vietnam (and in Cambodia and Laos and South Vietnam), the Communist jailers had ready recourse to unthinkable cruelty and brutality: solitary confinement, ritual humiliation, Cuban torture experts, and the withholding of medical treatment. The Americans had only a belief in God, family, and country; a strong tradition of loyalty and devotion to their fellow men; and a vast supply of creativity, humor, inventiveness, physical courage, and character. They could not be defeated by their North Vietnamese jailers. Three Americans—Jim Stockdale, Bud Day, and Lance Sijan—received the Congressional Medal of Honor for their actions in the face of this pitiless enemy.

Certainly the North Vietnamese "broke" a number of the POWs with their torture techniques. There are no concrete defenses against pain being inflicted to the point where the mind cannot control actions. But the North Vietnamese obtained no military information of any significant use to them. The torture was often increased when the humiliated North Vietnamese interrogators found out that Mickey Mouse didn't command the 7th Fleet or that Huckleberry Finn was not gathering intelligence in Hanoi. The Vietnamese method of torture emphasized the infliction of excruciating, debilitating, and mind-destroying pain, going far beyond what most people can imagine. The alleged "confessions" of pilots targeting hospitals and orphanages could only be taken seriously by America-haters.

One example of what a POW could expect comes from the book *Honor Bound* about the experiences of Americans captured by the Communists. The man described below is Air Force Captain Earl Cobeil:

The man could barely walk; he shuffled slowly, painfully. His clothes were torn to shreds. He was bleeding everywhere, terribly swollen, and a dirty, yellowish black and purple from head to toe. The man's head was down; he made no attempt to look at anyone.... Fidel [the Cuban torturer brought in by the North Vietnamese] smashed his fist into the man's face, driving him against the wall. Then he was brought to the center of the room and made to get down onto his knees. Screaming in rage, Fidel took a length of black rubber hose from a guard and lashed it as hard as he could into the man's face. The prisoner did not react; he did not cry out or even blink an eye. His failure to react seemed to fuel Fidel's rage and again he whipped the rubber hose across the man's face....[3]

After Fidel and the guards left the cell, Cobeil's cellmate found that Cobeil "had been through much more than the day's beatings. His body was ripped and torn everywhere; 'hell cuffs' appeared almost to have severed the wrists; strap marks still wound around the arms all the way to the shoulders; slivers of bamboo were embedded in the bloodied shins and there were what appeared to be tread marks from the hose across the chest, back and legs."[4]

I have been privileged to know a number of the American POWs. Mike Cronin was a classmate in flight school. Joe Mobley is a close friend, and he honored my son by

Communist Cruelty

It has been suggested that the POWs in Hanoi would have received better treatment if the United States had formally declared war on North Vietnam. Alas, Hanoi's treatment of Americans in their prisons *was* criminal, even without invoking international conventions on the treatment of prisoners of war. Hanoi was cruel to its own citizens; it was cruel to our citizens; *law* and *human rights* are bourgeois concepts for which the Communists in Hanoi had little respect.

attending his graduation from Marine boot camp. Robbie Risner has been a friend of the family for decades. He is one of the finest men I have ever known. His devotion to God and country sets a standard for all Americans. His gentleness and kindness belie his past as a fighter ace in Korea. His lack of bitterness and his peace of mind are humbling, knowing that he was one of the most tortured of all American POWs in the Vietnam War. At the retirement ceremony for General Risner—hosted by H. Ross Perot, whose efforts on behalf of the POWs and their families are unparalleled—I was able to chat with Jerry Denton, Jim Stockdale, Red McDaniel, John McCain, and dozens of others, including many of the Son Tay Raiders. America has no finer men.

Vietnam Veteran—and proud of it

Of course, few veterans were POWs. For most of us—the vast majority of us—reentering civilian life was easy. By every socio-economic measure—income, marriage success, advanced education, psychological health, lack of drug usage, avoiding prison—Vietnam Veterans exceed their non-military peers—just about the exact opposite of what the popular culture would like you to believe.[9]

To me, that's not surprising. We put the war behind us as best we could and entered the American mainstream. We were armed with something that increasingly few Americans were privileged to have—the knowledge that we had served our country. If freedom has a price, we and our colleagues had paid it. We recognized life and freedom as precious gifts. Some of us became famous—like football superstar Roger Staubach, or Federal Express Founder Fred Smith, or Senator John McCain, or game-show host Pat Sajak—but most of us were content to lead normal, everyday American lives, working hard and raising families.

The myth that Vietnam Veterans are racked with guilt and nightmares and angst, disproportionately prone to violence and drug use, and unable to easily fit into society, tenaciously survives despite the fact that statistics available from hundreds of sources—veterans groups, the VA, the Department of Defense, studies by scores of universities, and more—utterly disprove it. So why should this myth—and it is a shameful myth, besmirching a generation—survive?

Well, I'd say it survives because it makes liberals feel good. If you want to believe that the Vietnam War was an immoral and unnecessary war, it's awfully convenient to say that those who fought the war were traumatized by it. It makes it seem like you care about veterans—you feel so sorry for them—while simultaneously asserting that anti-war protesters were actually right about the war and are certainly better adjusted than those who served their country. And of course, for men who might in their heart of hearts wonder whether they were cowards because they didn't serve, the myth of the troubled veteran is awfully comforting.

The pernicious myths about Vietnam veterans have meant that almost every one of us has had to spend time explaining what we didn't do in the war. It has meant that most veteran fathers have had anxious moments knowing their children were being told lies and exaggerations about the war. And it has meant that most of us have had to put up with what amounts to a nasty little prejudice. On more than one occasion after returning from Southeast Asia in 1970, it was suggested to this author that he downplay his Vietnam service on his resume. When asked why, the employment recruiters replied, "Well—you know."

Books the Viet Cong Wouldn't Want You to Read

The Passing of the Night: My Seven Years as a Prisoner of the North Vietnamese, Robbie Risner[5]

A Code to Keep: The True Story of America's Longest Held Civilian Prisoner of War in Vietnam, Ernie Brace[6]

Prisoner at War: The Survival of Commander Richard A. Stratton, Scott Blakey[7]

Solitary Survivor: The First American POW in Southeast Asia, Lawrence Bailey[8]

What we should all know is that the men who served in Vietnam were the best educated, best trained, and most successful (in terms of kill ratio) army that the United States had deployed to that time. Under the most trying conditions, with, at times, dubious leadership, and a ques-

Vietnam War Movies

Apocalypse Now—War can certainly seem surreal and disorienting, but this film goes, shall we say, a bit over the top in its stereotypes and silliness. It's supposed to be "art," but it's not to be taken seriously. But to be honest, I kind of like it. There is a certain zaniness to it that does mirror the Vietnam War, and all wars, to a degree. After all, grown men are trying to shoot one another. Like most Vietnam War movies, however, it just forgets who the good guys were.

Coming Home—Forget that you hate Jane Fonda (come on, try), forget that she spends most of the movie spouting inane pseudo political statements, forget that most people saw the movie because of an unfortunate sex scene (it was a period where, to filmmakers at least, this seemed very brave). Actually, you can forget the movie, but it does have a moment or two. A twelve-hour flight from the jungles of Vietnam into the suburban environs of America was the most disorienting event of most Vietnam veterans' lives. The film deals with it, kind of. Unfortunately, the airhead Fonda had to make it a "statement" on the "morality" of the war—in the midst of an adulterous relationship, of course.

The Deer Hunter—The first half of the movie, in the Pennsylvania hometown of the three protagonists preparing to go to Vietnam, is roughly as long as the actual war. Or at least it seems that way. But if you have the stamina for it, it's not a bad movie.

tionable strategy, they defeated a merciless army that enjoyed unlimited support from its Communist allies. Though veterans came home to a country that was full of protesters who were likely to revile them, they excelled on their return to private life. All armies have their misfits,

---

Full Metal Jacket—It screws up its first half by attaching a psychopathic scene to what had been a fairly realistic look at Marine Corps boot camp. It ruins the second half (in country) by closing with a little anti-war sermon.

The Green Berets—Basically a World War II movie transferred to a not-very-Vietnam-looking Vietnam. At least its heart is in the right place.

Hamburger Hill—The story of the 101st Airborne taking Hill 937 in one of the last big battles of the war. Forget trying to read any political statements into the action. The film once again depicts the gut-wrenching horror of ground combat.

The Hanoi Hilton—A good, well-intentioned movie about life in the prisons of North Vietnam that, perhaps for reasons of decency, avoids exposing the depths of the brutality of the North Vietnamese guards and torture specialists.

Platoon—Okay, the bad American soldiers are rednecks and drink beer. They treat the Vietnamese people like dirt. The good American soldiers smoke dope. They treat the Vietnamese people with compassion. And the movie was made by Oliver Stone. With that out of the way, at least some of the combat scenes are realistic.

We Were Soldiers—The battle the 7th Cavalry fought in the Ia Drang Valley, led by Colonel Hal Moore. Just a darn good flick. Realistic combat and superb acting. Makes you proud.

---

malingerers, screw-ups, and complainers (we had John Kerry, after all), but they were just that—misfits, a small minority. And despite all the abuse that has been heaped upon the Vietnam veteran, the American people know better. Polling shows that there is an overwhelming respect for Vietnam veterans—even to a comical degree. For instance, the August 2000 census found that 13 million Americans falsely claimed to be Vietnam Veterans. It seems we have some cachet.

The best books about the war (an impossible list)

(N=Non-Fiction; F=Fiction)

I am approaching 300 books written about the Vietnam War in my personal library. There is no true *best* list that I could construct. The following list attempts to address different views and time periods.

- *A Better War: The Unexamined Victories and Final Tragedy of America's Last Years in Vietnam*, Lewis Sorely (Harcourt, 1999) (N)—A clear-eyed, well-focused view of the last five years of the war.
- *A Rumor of War*, Philip Caputo (Holt, Rinehart, Winston, 1977) (F)—A Marine lieutenant's view of combat. Thoughtful and well-written. Too true to be fiction.
- *Big Victory, Great Task*, General Vo Nguyen Giap (Frederick A. Praeger, 1968) (N/F) The "great" general's musings and illusions about beating the Americans. Propaganda as history.
- *Big Story*, Peter Braestrup (Yale University Press, 1977) (N)—An invaluable account of the media in Vietnam.
- *Don't Tread on Me*, H. W. Crocker III (Crown Forum, 2006) (N)—No book puts the Vietnam War in better perspective than this dynamic and well-written survey of all of America's

wars. It should be required reading in high school and college American history classes (not likely).

- *Fields of Fire*, James Webb (Prentice-Hall, Inc., 1978) (F)—Another Marine lieutenant. Maybe the best novel to come out of the war.

- *Hell in a Very Small Place*, Bernard Fall (Vintage Press, 1966) (N)—If you want to know about Dien Bien Phu, read this. A great book on war, strategy, hubris, and tragedy.

- *Honor Bound; American Prisoners of War in Southeast Asia 1961-1973,* Stuart I. Rochester and Frederick Kiley (Naval Institute Press, 1999) (N)—The story of the American POWs. Brutal and moving.

- *In the Jaws of History*, Bui Diem (Indiana University Press, 1999) (N)— A memoir of the war by a high-ranking South Vietnamese official. Read what someone who is unabashedly pro-American thinks about the United States cutting and running, leaving his country to the Communists.

- *Jane Fonda's War*, Mary Hershberger (The New Press, 2005) (N?)—"Everyone needs to read this story of the movie star who chose to use her fame to speak out against a barbaric and criminal war" (Mark Kurlansky, from the jacket). Problem is, she spoke out in *support* of those perpetrating barbaric criminal acts—the North Vietnamese. Conservatives and thoughtful liberals who read will either laugh—or cry.

- *Lost Victory*, William E. Colby (Contemporary Books, Inc., 1989) (N)—The former CIA director was there, he saw, and he wrote. More thoughtful and insightful than you might think a CIA proponent of the war might be.

- *On Yankee Station,* John B. Nichols and Barrett Tillman (Naval Institute Press, 1987) (N)—What was it like to fly into North Vietnam off a carrier? Read this, and also find out why the "Top Gun" fighter school was started by the U.S. Navy.

- *Small Unit Action in Vietnam*, Capt. Francis J. West, Jr. (Arno Press, Inc., 1967) (N)—Proof that it doesn't have to be long to be good, this is a great book. Yes, by a Marine again. A brilliant book (once printed as a tactical lesson aid). Want to know what it was like to be on a Marine patrol in Vietnam in 1966? This is the book to read.

- *Stolen Valor*, B. G. Burkett and Glenna Whitley (Verity Press, 1998) (N)—A pretty full account of what the anti-war crowd and media cost the American Vietnam War Veteran. Should be required reading in American schools (not likely).

- *Street Without Joy*, Bernard Fall (Pall Mall Press, 1964). (N)—Lessons we might have learned, but didn't.

- *The First Battle*, Otto N. Lehrack (Casemate, 2004) (N)—The wake-up call for the Marines in Vietnam in 1965.

- *The Lands of Charm and Cruelty*, Stan Sesser (Alfred A. Knopf, 1993) (N)—Okay, not about the war. But if you don't know squat about Southeast Asia, then or now, you should read this great book. Stan Sesser writes about his travels after the war. Everyone should read him.

- *The Only War We've Got,* Daniel Ford (IUniverse, 2001)— Early war and spot on. One of the best to give a feel for the war from the beginnings.

- *The Pentagon Papers—The New York Times* (Bantam Books, 1971) (N)—Start with the cover: "Based on Investigative Reporting by Neil Sheehan." Yes, he was investigating secret U.S. government documents stolen and given to him by Daniel Ellsberg. An important book about the Vietnam War— but not for the reason that the *New York Times* seemed to believe. It is *not* about the evil machinations of an out-of-control Department of Defense and White House. It actually shows the uncertainty and thoughtfulness of those trying to plan a "limited war." Always keep in mind that the book is an interpretation of the actual documents, with a heavily anti-war bias. No one has ever read the entire 7,000-page stack of stolen documents and maintained their sanity.

- *The Ravens*, Christopher Robbins (Crown, 1987) (N)—The U.S. Air Force cowboys in Laos.

- *The Quiet American,* Graham Greene (Viking Press, 1956) (F)—A little known, and completely forgettable, fact is that this is the book that spawned my novel *Nam-A-Rama.* About the early involvement of America in Vietnam, yes.

Signs, Signs, Everywhere Are Signs

When Almost Captain Gearheardt (USMC) infiltrated the anti-war movement at Berkeley in the mid-1960s on behalf of the CIA—which was illegal, so he really didn't do it (for the record), but actually did it—he made signs for the demonstrators saying, "Support Communist Aggression" and "Abandon Our Allies" and "I'm Just Trying to Save My Ass," but none were carried by the Berkeley crowd. Gearheardt's own sign "Free Love Available Here" was knocked out of his hands by a brace of angry women in Che tee-shirts. Finally, he just made a sign that read "I Don't Support Evil Corrupt Government" and the demonstration was forgotten as everyone debated which government he was talking about.

About the feel, sights, and sounds of living in Vietnam, absolutely. In the foreword, Greene quotes Lord Byron:

> "This is the patent age of new inventions
> For killing bodies, and for saving souls,
> All propagated with the best intentions."

- *Triumph Forsaken*, Mark Moyar (Cambridge University Press, 2006) (N)—Best researched book about the Vietnam War written to date. It should be the textbook. Moyar will bring out a continuation of the incredibly thoroughly documented account soon. Get it and read it.
- *Vietnam at War*, Phillip B. Davidson (Oxford University Press, 1991) (N)—Very readable history of the war from a general who was a part of it.
- *Why We Were in Vietnam*, Norman Podhoretz (Simon and Schuster, 1982) (N)—That's the title and that's what it tells you. One of the very best.

This list is by no means exhaustive, nor is it meant to be representative. Only in the axe-grinding books of liberal extremists does the American military come across as anything but the finest army the world had ever seen.

Summing up: Lessons learned

To wrap things up, the author interviewed two of the most articulate veterans he knows, Marine Almost Captains Gerard Gearheardt and Jack Armstrong (they were selected for promotion from Lieutenant, but the paperwork was eaten by a Lance Corporal), to get their views on America's efforts in Vietnam. A-Captain Gearheardt is a sarcastic wise-guy, a founding member of the Youth for CIA movement. A-Captain Armstrong is more contemplative, and was an officer in his Methodist Youth Fellowship.

They are best friends and served in Vietnam in 1965 and 1966 as characters in a black comedy novel, *Nam-A-Rama*, often referred to as "the one that isn't as good as *Catch-22*."

Author: Gentlemen, I understand that you were once on a mission to stop the war in Vietnam. Could you tell me—

Gearheardt: We're not telling you a damn thing until we see some I.D.

Armstrong: Back off, Gearheardt. This is the guy that wrote our book.

Gearheardt: In that case, we were on a mission to do something that had to do with killing someone to stop something, but we didn't have enough bullets and the President chickened out and started dating some bar girl in the Philippines before—

Jack: Can it, Gearheardt.

Author: So you would say, Jack, that your mission in Vietnam was less than clear.

Jack: It was clear that we needed to stop the Communists—

Gearheardt: The rotten bastards.

Jack (cont):—but beyond killing a lot of them, it was difficult to see how it would all work out. Even at the rate we were killing them, it would have taken about eighty or so years to get them all dead.

Gearheardt: And worth every minute of it.

Author: Wasn't it the theory that they would suffer so many losses they would surrender?

Gearheardt: Ha. Good one.

Author: No, seriously, the idea was that it would become so painful that—

Jack: Well, you would have thought that someone in D.C. noticed that Mao lost fifty or sixty million folks and didn't break down in tears or anything. Of course, he had a few hundred million left. Ho probably thought he could borrow some peasants if he ran out of people willing to be slaughtered.

Gearheardt: Wasn't like he was running for re-election or anything.

Author: So the U.S. military just couldn't get the job done with the weapons we had? Is that it?

Jack: It kind of turned into a "he said—she said" situation. We whipped the Commies at Tet in 1969 but the Commies said we didn't. The leftists and most of the media in America believed the Commies.

Author: Why was that?

Jack: Simple. The press claimed we told them the war was over in 1967 and they got burned when the Viet Cong committed mass suicide at Tet 1968. So Walter Cronkite did a ten day study of the war, ignoring the 50,000 or so dead Viet Cong, and said "Yep, no way we can beat these guys."

Gearheardt: Yeah. The press asked the American people, "Who you gonna believe, the Commies or that lying Department of Defense?" My theory is that Cronkite got the Saigon shuffle from a dirty rice bowl and just said to hell with the whole thing.

Author: So what happened? I mean after Tet.

Jack: Unfortunately, LBJ believed the press too. So he threw in the towel. Left things wide open for Dick and Curley.

Author: You mean Nixon and Kissinger? What about them?

Gearheardt: Rode into town on a horse with one eye.

Jack: Gearheardt, what in the hell does that mean?

Gearheardt: Old cowboy expression, Jack. Means they were tough hombres. Nixon once said "I'm going to bomb those bastards like they've never been bombed before." The military just about wet their pants with glee. I know I did. Rumor has it the Joint Chiefs sacrificed a water buffalo in the basement. But I'm—

Jack: Don't mind him. The deal is that Nixon came into office in 1969 and just went berserk. Put a new team in Saigon that started working with the South Vietnamese to take back the countryside. Started bombing the sanctuaries the enemy had in Cambodia. Bombed the crap out of the enemy when they violated the agreements. Started secret negotiations to end the war. And, if you can believe this, started withdrawing American troops. Just went nuts.

Author: That was berserk?

Gearheardt: I can only assume lots of the anti-war folks had big money on the Cong.

Jack: We just whipped their butts every time they showed up. The ARVN could pretty well handle them on the ground as long as the U.S. pulverized them from the air. We didn't really even need to leave ground troops there, like we did in Korea and Germany.

Liberal Lexicon

"If supporters of U.S. wars who didn't personally fight are, as the Left likes to say, 'chickenhawks,' does that mean that Lefties who dodged the draft are 'chickensh-ts'?"

—G. Gearheardt,
Almost Captain, USMC
Retired

Author: I'm not sure I get what was so "nuts" about that. It seems like what we should have been doing.

Gearheardt: You'll never get into Congress with that attitude. Not on the liberal ticket anyway.

Author: So what happened?

Jack: By late 1972 the commies were running out of fresh cannon fodder—they had plenty in the feedlot back home, but none to send to slaughter right then—and the negotiators had eaten all the rich French food they could handle, so they agreed to a cease fire.

Author: That was it?

Jack: Well, the commies threw one last temper tantrum but Jolly Saint Nixon painted a B-52 red, loaded some five hundred pounders in a tote bag, and paid Hanoi an early Christmas visit in 1972.

Gearheardt: The paintjob was my idea.

Author: And a good one.

Gearheardt: So, after U.S. airpower ground Hanoi and Haiphong into pretty much looking like they did before the bombing started, the Commies scrambled back to Paris and signed. They had lost maybe a million troops in the past ten years, but after 1,300 people were killed at Christmas—you know how those commies get all sentimental around Christ's birthday—they pulled an LBJ. Threw in the towel. Signed a peace treaty.

Jack: The U.S. government pretended they meant to abide by it! But the commies had a reputation to live up to. In the past hundred years they had never **not** broken a treaty. They damn sure weren't going to start now.

Author: Wait a minute. The North Vietnamese had no intention of living up to the Paris agreements?

Gearheardt: Ha. Another good one. You're a regular Abbot and Costello. They just needed some time to rebuild their weapon stash, recruit a few more farm boys, and consult with the Rooskies and the Reds in Beijing. I guess they still called it Peiping then.

Jack: Peking.

Vietnam Veterans: Unsung Heroes

"Dropped onto the enemy's terrain 12,000 miles away from home, America's citizen-soldiers performed with a tenacity and quality that may never be truly understood. Those who believe the war was fought incompletely on a tactical level should consider Hanoi's recent admission that 1.4 million of its soldiers died on the battlefield, compared to 58,000 total U.S. dead. Those who believe that it was a "dirty little war" where the bombs did all the work might contemplate that it was the most costly war the U.S. Marine Corps has ever fought—five times as many dead as World War I, three times as many dead as in Korea, and more total killed and wounded than in all of World War II....To this day it stuns me that their own countrymen have so completely missed the story of their service, lost in the bitter confusion of the war itself."[10]

—**Senator James Webb of Virginia,** former Secretary of the Navy, and Marine veteran of the Vietnam War (for which service he was awarded the Navy Cross, Silver Star, and Bronze Star medals for heroism)

Gearheardt: Nixon told them, and the South Vietnamese who were scared shi—

Jack: Family book, Gearheardt.

Gearheardt:—scared to death, that the U.S. would come back and bomb the crap out of them if they tried anything. They hated Nixon and were afraid of him. He had just spoiled their Christmas.

Author: So in early 1973 the U.S. had its troops out, had a cease fire, and the government in Saigon was still in charge. What happened?

Jack: The only people who hated Nixon more than the North Vietnamese were the Democrats in Congress. So they pulled the rug out from under his plan. Voted to stop all air support and cut the funding back to breech-loaders and fist-sized rocks. The North Vietnamese attacked a village or two. Congress impeached Nixon in retaliation. So the North Vietnamese blasted their way down to Saigon and took over.

Gearheardt: Yeah, the last shipment of weapons we sent to the South Vietnamese were those little rifles that shot out a flag that said "Bang" when you pulled the trigger. The North Vietnamese were so sure that the U.S. wouldn't do anything to stop them that they sent every soldier they had down south. They had old guys with sticks guarding Hanoi. I could've taken Hanoi with a troop of Lithuanian Girl Scouts.

Author: So that was it? We just bugged out after we had beaten them on the battlefield?

Gearheardt: Oh, I think we threatened to send Ted Kennedy over to rampage through the Hanoi bars, but it was all over. We fought Communism to a halt in Vietnam but couldn't defeat weaselism in our own back yard. The pink-libs spouted a feedlot full of bull crap about the morality of the war, and how hard it was to fight, and why we needed the money to deliver a pig to every pot in America or some socialist rant, and that was pretty much it. A sad day for America. Sadder for twenty million South Vietnamese, of course.

Author: Hmmm. Did we learn anything? What did it all mean?

Jack: Before Gearheardt starts into his anti-anti-war tirade and how it affected us in Iraq, let me try to answer that.

Gearheardt: To heck with you, Jack. We should've rounded up those draft-dodging, lily-livered, Communist sympathizers—did you know some of them actually supported the enemy for Pete's sake?—and sent them to a penal colony or France or somewhere. That's another thing wrong with America these days—

Jack: Calm down, Gearheardt. Look, here's the thing. I'll run through a list of *issues* we encountered and you stop me when I mention one that we *needed* to learn: War is brutal. Limited war is an oxymoron. Communists lie. Communists don't understand the concept of attrition. War is expensive. *Stopping* the bombing of someone doesn't encourage them to surrender. A new government in a country under siege might not be real stable. Asian leaders aren't Democrats. Some people don't like the idea of going to a foreign land and getting shot. Some people don't like war at all. It's not a good idea to give an enemy a "King's X" place where you can't shoot at them. It's a bad idea for your own media to broadcast enemy propaganda as news. South Vietnamese soldiers aren't as good as the best trained, best equipped, most educated soldiers in the history of warfare.

Author: I think I get your drift. So we really didn't learn anything?

Jack: What was there to learn?

Gearheardt: Tell him your *Jack Rule*, Jack.

Jack: It's just this. At the end of every meeting for planning a war, the last question asked should always be, "Does this make any sense?" Apparently it was never asked until Nixon took office.

Author: So nothing was accomplished?

Jack: I didn't say that. Gearheardt and I are just Marines, Almost Captains. We were asked to go kill a lot of Viet Cong and NVA soldiers so they would stop murdering and kidnapping South Vietnamese villagers, and trying to overthrow the government, then chase their butts back to their home. We did that. We didn't go over there to *learn* anything.

Gearheardt: The enemy learned they could manipulate the U.S. media and the anti-war crowd. That was a good lesson. Hopefully we'll never have another unpopular war.

All: Ha Ha Ha.

ACKNOWLEDGMENTS

This book would have not been possible without an incredible amount of hard work, research, sweat, and toil. Fortunately, I didn't have to do any of it.

In addition to having an editor (the esteemed Harry Crocker) who knew the subject better than I did, the research and work had already been done by brilliant writers, historians and essayists like Mark Moyar (a very special thanks), David Phillips, Norman Podhoretz, Pat Buchanan, William E. Colby, Bing West, Bernard Fall, and dozens of historians and journalists, too numerous to mention here (I have included many more of them in the bibliography at the end of the book. I pray that I have given them sufficient attribution.)

I bear no ill will against the majority of those who protested the war (among whom I count a number of friends—until publication). Even the amnesty for draft-dodgers should be viewed in the context of the times. My willingness to forgive is not a matter of magnanimity on my part, but the balancing fact of gratefulness for having been given the opportunity to serve my country, help those in great need and danger, and experience a camaraderie rarely gained in life's endeavors. I actually feel sorry for those who chose not to serve for spurious reasons. The irony is that the majority of veterans, me included, feel they did nothing special. Their country asked—they responded. Serving alongside some of the finest

187

men I know—Lenny Porzio, Ramsey Myatt, Buddy Sanders, Dick Hooton, Bill Askins, Wayne Gentry, John Butler, and my other squadron mates—was a lasting gift.

One of the reasons people on the Left are so wrong about the Vietnam War is that they usually view the war in a highly parochial light—seeing it almost purely in terms of American domestic politics and a frankly ideological view of American history (in which Marxists are generally right and Americans, and our allies, and especially the United States military, are generally wrong). Very few ever bother to cite books written by South Vietnamese authors. But if you want to know what the United States was trying to protect South Vietnam from, read *Vietnam Under Communism, 1975-1982* by Nguyen Van Canh (Hoover Press, 1983).

It would, however, be hypocritical of me to pretend that I knew all the nuances and critical issues surrounding the Vietnam War when I was there as a young Lieutenant in the Marine Corps. I made a serious effort to know, but youth has its limits. Still, there was never any doubt in my mind when I was fighting alongside the South Vietnamese, South Koreans, Australians, and my fellow Americans that we were on the right side of the war, that the South Vietnamese people were generous, kind, and deserving, that our victory would mean a better future for them, and that the Communist soldiers were brutal opponents fighting for a hopeless and dark society.

This *Politically Incorrect Guide™ to the Vietnam War* is written with the hope (and confidence) that common sense and reasonableness based on fact will prove that America embarked on a noble cause, that we and our allies fought with magnificent valor, and that we presented the United States Congress the opportunity to inflict a decisive defeat on the North Vietnamese Communists. What Congress did with that opportunity is the true shame of the Vietnam War.

I'd like to thank Regnery (may they forever reign), Harry Crocker (again, and he deserves it), the lovely and patient Anneke Green (for whom my plea that "we don't need no stinking footnotes" cut no ice), and my equally patient agent, Deborah Grosvenor. On the home front, my gratitude to son Jason (whose independent thought I greatly admire), daughter Alison (whose persistence in her career I also admire), son 2nd Lt. Coleman, USMC (whose career choice is a constant inspiration), and, of course, wife Deborah (who lived the war again this past year or more whilst I ignored hearth and home). God Bless Them All. And God Bless the men and women of the military current. As they protect our way of life by risking theirs, I pray they see through the shameful political shenanigans in the nation's (and world's) capital, and realize their service is vital and infinitely respected by those who matter.

Cheers,

PEJ

REMARKS OF SENATOR JOHN F. KENNEDY AT THE CONFERENCE ON VIETNAM

Luncheon in the Hotel Willard, Washington, D.C., June 1, 1956

It is a genuine pleasure to be here today at this vital Conference on the future of Vietnam, and America's stake in that new nation, sponsored by the American Friends of Vietnam, an organization of which I am proud to be a member. Your meeting today at a time when political events concerning Vietnam are approaching a climax, both in that country and in our own Congress, is most timely. Your topic and deliberations, which emphasize the promise of the future more than the failures of the past, are most constructive. I can assure you that the Congress of the United States will give considerable weight to your findings and recommendations; and I extend to all of you who have made the effort to participate in this Conference my congratulations and best wishes.

It is an ironic and tragic fact that this Conference is being held at a time when the news about Vietnam has virtually disappeared from the front pages of the American press, and the American people have all but forgotten the tiny nation for which we are in large measure responsible. This decline in public attention is due, I believe, to three factors: (1) First, it is due in part to the amazing success of President Diem in meeting firmly and with determination the major political and economic crises which had heretofore continually plagued Vietnam. (I shall say more about this point later, for it deserves more consideration from all Americans interested in the future of Asia.)

(2) Secondly, it is due in part to the traditional role of American journalism, including readers as well as writers, to be more interested in crises than in accomplishments, to give more space to the threat of wars than the need for works, and to write larger headlines on the sensational omissions of the past than the creative missions of the future.

(3) Third and finally, our neglect of Vietnam is the result of one of the most serious weaknesses that has hampered the long-range effectiveness of American foreign policy over the past several years—and that is the over emphasis upon our role as "volunteer fire department" for the world. Whenever and wherever fire breaks out—in Indo-China, in the Middle East, in Guatemala, in Cyprus, in the Formosan Straits—our firemen rush in, wheeling up all their heavy equipment, and resorting to every known method of containing and extinguishing the blaze. The crowd gathers—the usually successful efforts of our able volunteers are heartily applauded—and then the firemen rush off to the next conflagration, leaving the grateful but still stunned inhabitants to clean up the rubble, pick up the pieces and rebuild their homes with whatever resources are available.

The role, to be sure, is a necessary one; but it is not the only role to be played, and the others cannot be ignored. A volunteer fire department halts, but rarely prevents, fires. It repels but rarely rebuilds; it meets the problems of the present but not of the future. And while we are devoting our attention to the Communist arson in Korea, there is smoldering in Indo-China; we turn our efforts to Indo-China until the alarm sounds in Algeria—and so it goes.

Of course Vietnam is not completely forgotten by our policy-makers today—I could not in honesty make such a charge and the facts would easily refute it—but the unfortunate truth of the matter is that, in my opinion, Vietnam would in all likelihood be receiving more attention from our Congress and Administration, and greater assistance under our aid programs, if it were in imminent danger of Communist invasion or revolution. Like those peoples of Latin America and Africa whom we have very nearly overlooked in the past decade, the Vietnamese may find that their devotion to the cause of democracy, and their success in reducing the strength of local Communist groups, have had the ironic effect of reducing American support. Yet the need for that support has in no way been reduced. (I hope it will not be necessary for the Diem Government—or this organization—to subsidize the growth of the South Vietnam Communist Party in order to focus American attention on that nation's critical needs!)

No one contends that we should now rush all our firefighting equipment to Vietnam, ignoring the Middle East or any other part of the world. But neither should we conclude that the cessation of hostilities in Indo-China removed that area from the list of important areas of United States foreign policy. Let us briefly consider exactly what is "America's Stake in Vietnam":

(1) First, Vietnam represents the cornerstone of the Free World in Southeast Asia, the keystone to the arch, the finger in the dike. Burma, Thailand, India, Japan, the Philippines and obviously Laos and Cambodia are among those whose security would be threatened if the Red Tide of Communism overflowed into Vietnam. In the past, our policy-makers have sometimes issued contradictory statements on this point—but the long history of Chinese invasions of Southeast Asia being stopped by Vietnamese warriors should have removed all doubt on this subject.

Moreover, the independence of a Free Vietnam is crucial to the free world in fields other than the military. Her economy is essential to the economy of Southeast Asia; and her political liberty is an inspiration to those seeking to obtain or maintain their liberty in all parts of Asia—and indeed the world. The fundamental tenets of this nation's foreign policy, in short, depend in considerable measure upon a strong and free Vietnamese nation.

(2) Secondly, Vietnam represents a proving ground of democracy in Asia. However we may choose to ignore it or deprecate it, the rising prestige and influence of Communist China in Asia are unchallengable facts. Vietnam represents the alternative to Communist dictatorship. If this democratic experiment fails, if some one million refugees have fled the totalitarianism of the North only to find neither freedom nor security in the South, then weakness, not strength, will characterize the meaning of democracy in the minds of still more Asians. The United States is directly responsible for this experiment—it is playing an important role in the laboratory where it is being conducted. We cannot afford to permit that experiment to fail.

(3) Third and in somewhat similar fashion, Vietnam represents a test of American responsibility and determination in Asia. If we are not the parents of little Vietnam, then surely we are the godparents. We presided at its birth, we gave assistance to its life, we have helped to shape its future. As French influence in the political, economic and military spheres has declined in Vietnam, American influence has steadily grown. This is our offspring—we cannot abandon it, we cannot ignore its needs. And if it falls victim to any of the perils that threaten its existence—Communism, political anarchy, poverty and the rest—then the United States, with some justification, will be held responsible; and our prestige in Asia will sink to a new low.

(4) Fourth and finally, America's stake in Vietnam, in her strength and in her security, is a very selfish one—for it can be measured, in the last analysis, in terms of American lives and American dollars. It is now well known that we were at one time on the brink of war in Indo-china—a

war which could well have been more costly, more exhausting and less conclusive than any war we have ever known. The threat to such war is not now altogether removed form the horizon. Military weakness, political instability or economic failure in the new state of Vietnam could change almost overnight the apparent security which has increasingly characterized that area under the leadership of Premier Diem. And the key position of Vietnam in Southeast Asia, as already discussed, makes inevitable the involvement of this nation's security in any new outbreak of trouble.

It is these four points, in my opinion, that represent America's stake in Vietnamese security. And before we look to the future, let us stop to review what the Diem Government has already accomplished by way of increasing that security. Most striking of all, perhaps, has been the rehabilitation of more than 3/4 of a million refugees from the North. For these courageous people dedicated to the free way of life, approximately 45,000 houses have been constructed, 2,500 wells dug, 100 schools established and dozens of medical centers and maternity homes provided.

Equally impressive has been the increased solidarity and stability of the Government, the elimination of rebellious sects and the taking of the first vital steps toward true democracy. Where once colonialism and Communism struggled for supremacy, a free and independent republic has been proclaimed, recognized by over forty countries of the free world. Where once a playboy emperor ruled from a distant shore, a constituent assembly has been elected.

Social and economic reforms have likewise been remarkable. The living conditions of the peasants have been vastly improved, the wastelands have been cultivated, and a wider ownership of the land is gradually being encouraged. Farm cooperatives and farmer loans have modernized an outmoded agricultural economy; and a tremendous dam in the center of the country has made possible the irrigation of a vast area previously uncultivated. Legislation for better labor relations, health protection, working conditions and wages has been completed under the leadership of President Diem.

Finally, the Vietnamese army—now fighting for its own homeland and not its colonial masters—has increased tremendously in both quality and quantity. General O'Daniel can tell you more about these accomplishments.

But the responsibility of the United States for Vietnam does not conclude, obviously, with a review of what has been accomplished thus far with our help. Much more needs to be done; much more, in fact, than we have been doing up to now. Military alliances in Southeast Asia are necessary but not enough. Atomic superiority and the development of new ultimate weapons are not enough. Informational and propaganda activities, warning of the evils of Communism and the blessings of the American way of life, are not enough in a country where concepts of free enterprise and capitalism are meaningless, where poverty and hunger are not enemies across the 17th parallel but enemies within their midst. As Ambassador Chuong has recently said: "People cannot be expected to fight for the Free World unless they have their own freedom to defend, their freedom from foreign domination as well as freedom from misery, oppression, corruption."

I shall not attempt to set forth the details of the type of aid program this nation should offer the Vietnamese—for it is not the details of that program that are as important as the spirit with which it is offered and the objectives it seeks to accomplish. We should not attempt to buy the friendship of the Vietnamese. Nor can we win their hearts by making them dependent upon our handouts. What we must offer them is a revolution—a political, economic and social revolution far superior to anything the Communists can offer—far more peaceful, far more democratic and far more locally controlled. Such a Revolution will require much from the United States and much from Vietnam. We must supply capital to replace that drained by the centuries of colonial exploitation; technicians to train those handicapped by deliberate policies of illiteracy;

guidance to assist a nation taking those first feeble steps toward the complexities of a republican form of government. We must assist the inspiring growth of Vietnamese democracy and economy, including the complete integration of those refugees who gave up their homes and their belongings to seek freedom. We must provide military assistance to rebuild the new Vietnamese Army, which every day faces the growing peril of Vietminh Armies across the border.

And finally, in the councils of the world, we must never permit any diplomatic action adverse to this, one of the youngest members of the family of nations—and I include in that injunction a plea that the United States never give its approval to the early nationwide elections called for by the Geneva Agreement of 1954. Neither the United States nor Free Vietnam was a party to that agreement—and neither the United States nor Free Vietnam is ever going to be a party to an election obviously stacked and subverted in advance, urged upon us by those who have already broken their own pledges under the Agreement they now seek to enforce.

All this and more we can offer Free Vietnam, as it passes through the present period of transition on its way to a new era—an era of pride and independence, and era of democratic and economic growth—an era which, when contrasted with the long years of colonial oppression, will truly represent a political, social and economic revolution.

This is the revolution we can, we should, we must offer to the people of Vietnam—not as charity, not as a business proposition, not as a political maneuver, nor simply to enlist them as soldiers against Communism or as chattels of American foreign policy—but a revolution of their own making, for their own welfare, and for the security of freedom everywhere. The Communists offer them another kind of revolution, glittering and seductive in its superficial appeal. The choice between the two can be made only by the Vietnamese people themselves. But in these times of trial and burden, true friendships stand out. As Premier Diem recently wrote a great friend of Vietnam, Senator Mansfield, "It is only in winter that you can tell which trees are evergreen." And I am confident that if this nation demonstrates that it has not forgotten the people of Vietnam, the people of Vietnam will demonstrate that they have not forgotten us.

John F. Kennedy Presidential Library and Museum
www.jfklibrary.org
(accessed January 7, 2010)

Appendix B

THE POLITICALLY INCORRECT GUIDE TO THE PENTAGON PAPERS

THE MOST MISUNDERSTOOD DOCUMENT OF THE WAR

In 1967, Secretary of Defense Robert McNamara, the "architect of the Vietnam War," organized a study of the war's origins and conduct, based largely on documents held at the Pentagon. It took McNamara's team (The Vietnam Study Task Force) more than a year to produce what amounted to an encyclopedic, 7,000-page history of the Vietnam War. Its official title was *US—Vietnam Relations, 1945-1967: History of US Decision Making Process on Vietnam Policy.*

When Leslie Gelb, the director of the Pentagon project, wrote to LBJ's new Secretary of Defense, Clark Clifford, to inform him the work was completed, the letter included these inspiring observations: "The people who worked on the task force were superb—uniformly bright and interested, although not always versed in the art of research." And this, "We had a sense of doing something important and of the need to do it right. Of course, we all had our prejudices and axes to grind and these shine through clearly at times, but we tried, we think, to suppress them or compensate for them."

Today, this 7,000-page opus is better known as the "Pentagon Papers," the name affixed to it by the media when it was publicized in 1971—after Rand Corporation analyst Daniel Ellsberg leaked it. The *New York Times* decided to publish the papers, pared down to the most damning (in its

199

judgment) information, with analysis provided by the *Times'* reporters and editors.

The Pentagon Papers became a *cause célèbre* for the anti-war Left because their publication allowed the left to wrap itself in the mantle of free speech and freedom of the press, and because the Left had a perverse desire for what it thought might be damaging information about the U.S. government—even if that damaging information was about the Kennedy and Johnson administrations. But the effectiveness of the Pentagon Papers for the Left really depended on few people actually reading them, because in their totality, they provide nothing like the damning interpretation that the liberal media stamped on them.

What the Pentagon Papers show is how earnestly the United States government made the decision to go into Vietnam and how it searched diligently for the best way to prosecute and end the war. For the most part, the Pentagon Papers show reasonable, intelligent men, who had America's interests at heart, studying and debating about what to do in Indochina.

President Nixon was, at first, undisturbed that the *New York Times* had published the first installment of the Pentagon Papers. Henry Kissinger, however, reminded him that if these papers could be leaked and published, so could information about the administration's secret ongoing negotiations with North Vietnam, China, and the Soviet Union. Moreover, he said, the administration could not stand idly by and allow a precedent to be set that every angry dissenter from American policy could steal and publish secret government documents with impunity. Nixon agreed and acted. The government sued to prevent the publication. The case went before the Supreme Court.

The *New York Times* and *Washington Post* argued that the Pentagon Papers were historical and could have no influence on the conduct of the war or pose any risk to national security—(they argued this, while simultaneously arguing that it was absolutely necessary to put the Pentagon

Papers before the public as quickly as possible). No mention was made, understandably, of the desire to sell newspapers or provide ammunition for the anti-war Left (which was the side now taken by the *New York Times* and the *Washington Post*).

The Court ruled 6 to 3 in favor of the *New York Times* and *Washington Post*. Dissenting were Chief Justice Warren Burger, Harry Blackmun, and John Harlan. Justice Blackmun, in his dissent, reminded the Court that the "First Amendment, after all, is only one part of an entire Constitution. Article II of the great document vests in the Executive Branch primary power over the conduct of foreign affairs and places in that branch the responsibility for the Nation's safety. Each provision of the Constitution is important, and I cannot subscribe to a doctrine of unlimited absolutism for the First Amendment at the cost of downgrading other provisions."

Blackmun went on to note that "Justice Wilkey, dissenting in the District of Columbia case [dealing with the Pentagon Papers], after a review of only the affidavits before this Court (the basic papers had not been made available by either party), concluded that there were a number of examples of documents that, if in the possession of The *Post*, and if published, 'could clearly result in great harm to the nation,' and he defined harm to mean the 'death of soldiers, and destruction of alliances, the greatly increased difficulty of negotiation with our enemies, the inability of our diplomats to negotiate.'...I therefore share his concern. I hope that damage already has not been done. If, however, damage has been done, and if, with the Court's action today, these newspapers proceed to publish the critical documents and there results therefrom 'the death of soldiers, the destruction of alliances, the inability of our diplomats to negotiate' to which I might add the factors of prolongation of the war and of further delay in the freeing of United States prisoners, then the nation's people will know where the responsibility for these sad consequences rests."

One can say this with a certainty, the publication of the Pentagon Papers were certainly no help to the war effort, they provided great help to the anti-war movement (which used them to its own ends), and certainly added to an atmosphere in this country where it seemed as though the United States was rent by internal dissension, which certainly encouraged our enemies.

Motive? What motive?

If one gives the Bible to an atheist and is shocked by his analysis—that God is a pretty mean fellow, for example—then one might be shocked that the Pentagon Papers, given to anti-war reporter Neil Sheehan and the anti-war *New York Times*, were proclaimed to reveal a litany of lies, deceptions, and egregious criminal acts by the United States government.

The very first page of the *New York Times* book, *The Secret History of the Viet Nam War,* published in July 1971, angrily points out that Eisenhower, immediately after not signing (because he thought they were disastrous for South Vietnam) the Geneva accords of 1954—which called for a truce between the French and the Viet Minh and divided the country and set a date for "free elections"—sent a team of agents into North Vietnam who "spent the last days of [sic] Hanoi in contaminating the oil supply of the bus company for a gradual wreckage of engines in the buses, in taking actions for delayed sabotage of the railroad (which required teamwork with a CIA special technical team in Japan who performed their part brilliantly), and in writing detailed notes of potential targets for future para-military operations." They probably got away with it because Ho Chi Minh and his henchmen were busy slaughtering a few thousand peasants who had the audacity to own land or get an education. Nor were the Viet Minh being quiet during this period. They had, for instance, blown up large ammunition dumps at the Saigon airport. But for the *New York Times*, the scandal was that the United States government engaged in covert operations against the Communists. This was a government secret that simply had to be revealed to the public.

Another "shocker" revealed and mentioned in the introduction written by Sheehan, is the "absence of emotional anguish or moral questioning of action in the memorandums and cablegrams and records of the high-level policy discussions." First, that isn't actually true although the incidence is not frequent. Second, these are military and government documents. The concept of a good "group hug" had not been introduced into Pentagon strategy as yet. Is Sheehan suggesting that *prayer* should have been introduced into Pentagon or White House meetings? Not a bad idea necessarily, but liberals would then have protested about separation of church and state.

One of the complaints made about the Pentagon Papers was that the documents gave no *motive* for the actions discussed and taken. Plenty of goals, objectives, plans, suggestions, outlines, alternatives, and arguments were given, but no motives, which liberals, apparently, love to plumb.

If the Pentagon Papers don't contain motives and emotions, what *do* they contain? They contain a pretty good description and rationale for why we were in Vietnam, how things were going, and what our alternatives were. To read the Pentagon Papers (any version) and not get a fairly good idea of why we were in the war, you would have to be either (1) not very observant or (2) searching for a recitation of your own opinion of why we were there and not finding it. You could start with the National Security Council (NSC) 1952 Policy Study on Southeast Asia. Under the heading OBJECTIVE, it reads:

1. To prevent the countries of Southeast Asia from passing into the Communist orbit, and to assist them to develop will and ability to resist Communism from within and without and to contribute to the strengthening of the free world.

2. Communist domination, by whatever means, of all of Southeast Asia would seriously endanger in the short term, and critically endanger in the longer term, United States security interests.

Or maybe National Security Action Memorandum (NSAM) 52, signed by McGeorge Bundy on May 11, 1961:

1. The U.S. objective and concept of operations stated in report are approved: to prevent Communist domination of South Vietnam; to create in that country a viable and increasingly democratic society, and to initiate, on an accelerated basis, a series of mutually supporting actions of a military, political, economic, psychological and covert character designed to achieve this objective.

You might disagree with the objectives. Four administrations, Democrat and Republican, committed to the objectives. The Pentagon Papers are moot on their respective *motives.*

Paper chase

Hedrick Smith, in his foreword to the *New York Times* book on the Pentagon Papers, expresses surprise, disappointment, disbelief, and criticism that the papers do not provide conclusive answers to some of the "most widely asked questions about the war" such as:

- Precisely how was Ngo Dinh Diem returned to South Vietnam in 1954 from exile and helped to power? (*How widely asked was that? And the answer was pretty simple, Bao Dai needed a nationalist leader, and Diem's stock was rising in America, thanks in large part to conservative Catholics; it seemed like an opportune marriage.*)

- If President Kennedy had lived, would he have led the United States into a full-scale ground war in South Vietnam and an air war against North Vietnam as President Johnson did? (*Can anyone really have thought they might find the answer to an unknowable, hypothetical question in the Pentagon record? Really this is just a liberal wish, the desire to exculpate their hero from a war they deplore; the most one can guess about Kennedy, given his record, is that he would have been resolutely indecisive, opposed to Communist expansion in Indochina, and not at all certain what to do about it, but thinking he needed to do something.*)

- Did President Johnson's cutback of the bombing to the 20th Parallel on March 31, 1968, signal a lowering of American objectives for the war or was it merely an effort to buy more time and patience from a war-weary American public? (*In twenty-five words or less.*)

Hedrick Smith laments another omission: the absence of any extended discussion of military or political responsibility for such matters as civilian casualties or the restraints imposed by the rules of land warfare and the Geneva and Hague Conventions. Of course the overwhelming evidence showed that we avoided civilian casualties to the detriment of our own soldiers and airmen. As for the Geneva Convention, Mr. Hedrick Smith might not have known that all American soldiers, sailors, airmen, and Marines carried Geneva Convention cards with them, until they lost them or they turned to mush in the humidity or driving tropical rain. There were no lengthy discussions on prohibiting atrocities, because, well, you know, it was sort of assumed that everyone knew that atrocities are things we ought not to commit. Perhaps just to be safe, boats and aircraft carrying troops to Vietnam should have been outfitted with signage: Remember—No Atrocities.

In the first chapter of the *Times* book, reporter Fox Butterfield has a section titled "U.S. Policy in Disarray." No sense in being ambiguous. The second paragraph puts it all into perspective; American policy between 1940 and 1950, the study says, was "less purposeful" than most people have assumed, and more characterized by "ambivalence and indecision." I wonder: could it be that American policy on Indochina was indecisive, ambivalent, and less than purposeful because we happened to be fighting World War II and because after that we were rebuilding Europe and fighting the Korean War? That's just a wild guess.

The writer (of the Pentagon Papers, not the *Times* analyst analyzing the Pentagon Papers) goes on, quoting a cablegram sent by Secretary of State George C. Marshall to the embassy in Paris: "We have not fully recognized France's sovereign position and we do not wish to have it appear that we are in any way endeavoring undermining (sic) that position. At the same time we cannot shut our eyes to the fact that there are two sides to this problem and that our reports indicate both a lack of French understanding [of the] other side and [the] continued existence [of a] dangerously outmoded colonial outlook and method in areas. On the other hand we do not lose sight [of the] fact that Ho Chi Minh has direct Communist connections and it should be obvious that we are not interested in seeing colonial empire administrations supplanted by [the] philosophy and political organization directed from and controlled by [the] Kremlin. Frankly we have no solution of [the] problem to suggest." [End of cablegram]

To call this sentiment of George Marshall's, which reflects America's ambivalence about what to do in Indochina, an example of American foreign policy in "disarray" is pejorative at the very least. A more accurate description is that the United State wanted to find a Third Way between colonialism and Communism, one that would put the United States on the side of the nationalist aspirations of the people of Indochina. But we knew we needed to tread carefully, given the enormous threat and dan-

Such Good Friends

Was China a threat in the Vietnam War? It is unchallenged that China sent at least 50,000 troops to North Vietnam; some say the number was closer to 100,000; a few say 300,000. In Chinese schools in the late 1970s, it was taught that China won the Vietnam War against the Americans. (Of course, Vietnam and China then fought each other.)

ger of Communism. Rather than a policy in disarray, the United States had a policy of liberal idealism balanced with a realistic fear of Communist expansion.

The *New York Times* analysts of the Pentagon Papers made much of the alleged attempt by Ho Chi Minh to win American assistance against the French at the end of World War II. The analysts note that "from October 1945 until the following February, Ho sent eight letters to President Truman or his Secretary of State appealing for U.S. intervention against French colonialism. He supposedly received no reply."

Almost all critics of the American effort in Vietnam cite this episode as a "missed opportunity" to prevent the war and keep North Vietnam from becoming Communist. But a little reality check is needed. Ho Chi Minh was already a Communist. When the United States allied itself with Stalin to defeat Hitler, it did not make Stalin less of a Communist. If President Truman—who had other more pressing matters on his plate than writing to Ho Chi Minh—had thrown American support behind the Communists against the French, how would that have advanced American interests—or Vietnamese interests (if you think the Vietnamese people deserved better than life under Communism)?

Did the Pentagon Papers harm the war effort?

Given the strong suspicion that the *New York Times* and the *Washington Post* actually *intended* to harm the war effort, the answer might be in the eye of the beholder. Yet it is difficult to read the *New York Times* edition of the Pentagon Papers and not cringe, thinking that the enemy surely received a significant psychological boost from the publication, given that it was heralded as revealing embarrassing mistakes by the United States government. Here are some sections from the *Times* book.

"McNaughton Memo on Factors in Bombing Decision" (excerpts)

> We...have in Vietnam the ingredients of an enormous miscalculation.
>
> C. the present U.S. objective in Vietnam is to avoid humiliation. The reasons we went into Vietnam to the present depth are varied; but they are now largely academic. Why we have not withdrawn from Vietnam is, by all odds, one reason: (1) to preserve our reputation as a guarantor, and thus to preserve our effectiveness in the rest of the world. We have not hung on (2) to save a friend or (3) to deny the Communists the added acres and heads (because the dominoes don't fall for that reason in this case), or even (4) to prove that "wars of national liberation: won't work" (except as our reputation is involved).

> [And further in the memo]

"C. Future Bombing Strategy"

> Although bombings of North Vietnam improve GVN [government of South Vietnam] morale and provide a counter in eventual negotiations (should they take place) there is no evidence that they meaningfully reduce either the capacity or the will

for the DRV [government of North Vietnam] to support the VC [Viet Cong]. The DRV knows that we cannot force them to stop by bombing and that we cannot, without an unacceptable risk of a major war with China or Russia or both, force them to stop by conquering them or "blotting them out." Knowing that if they are not influenced we cannot stop them, the DRV will remain difficult to influence. With continuing DRV support, victory in the South may remain forever beyond our reach.

"Prime Minister Wilson's Warning to Johnson on Petroleum Raids" (excerpts)

I was most grateful to you for asking Bob McNamara to arrange the very full briefing about the two oil targets near Hanoi and Haiphong that Col. Rogers gave me yesterday....

I know that you will not feel that I am either unsympathetic or uncomprehending of the dilemma that this problem presents for you. In particular, I wholly understand the deep concern you must feel at the need to do anything possible to reduce the losses of young Americans in and over Vietnam; and Col. Rogers made it clear to us what care has been taken to plan this operation so as to keep civilian casualties to the minimum.

However...I am bound to say that, as seen from here, the possible military benefits that may result from this bombing do not appear to outweigh the political disadvantages that would seem the inevitable consequence. If you and the South Vietnamese Government were conducting a declared war on the conventional pattern...this operation would clearly be necessary and right. But since you have made it abundantly clear—and you know how much we have welcomed and supported this—that your purpose is to achieve a negotiated settlement, and that you are not striving for total military victory in the field, I remain convinced that the bombing of these targets, without producing decisive military advantage, may only increase the difficulty of reaching an eventual settlement....

The last thing I wish is to add to your difficulties, but, as I warned you in my previous message, if this action is taken we shall have to dissociate ourselves from it, and in doing so I should have to say that you had given me advance warning and that I had made my position clear to you....

Nevertheless I want to repeat...that our reservations about this operation will not affect our continuing support for your policy over Vietnam, as you and your people have made it clear from your Baltimore speech onwards. But, while this will remain the Government's position, I know the effect on public opinion in this country—and I believe throughout Western Europe—is likely to be such as to reinforce the existing disquiet and criticism that we have to deal with.

Someone should check and see if the entire NVA propaganda division got an extra bag of rice after the Pentagon Papers were published and spun by the *New York Times*. Or how many South Vietnamese caught the next flight out of Saigon. Perhaps no direct military secrets in the traditional sense were passed to the enemy in the Pentagon Papers. But certainly no thinking person in 1971 would be unaware that the Vietnam War was a war of wills for which the publication of the Pentagon Papers was at least a huge tactical victory for North Vietnam.

The *New York Times* published the Pentagon Papers to embarrass a government with which they did not agree. What they accomplished was to make Nixon and Kissinger's job of negotiating a peace with North Vietnam much harder. Nixon put it best, speaking to former POWs on March 24, 1973:

Ends and Means

A popular misunderstanding about the Vietnam War is that America did not have clearly defined goals. The answer to that is, ironically, found in what became the anti-war bible for the Left—The Pentagon Papers. The goals and objectives were clearly stated over and over again: an independent, free South Vietnam. It was how to achieve that, which was constantly, and in the Johnson years fruitlessly, debated.

Had we not had secrecy, had we not had secret negotiations with the North Vietnamese, had we not had secret negotiations prior to the Soviet summit, had we not had secret negotiations over a period of time with the Chinese leaders, let me say quite bluntly there would have been no China initiative, there would have been no limitations of arms for the Soviet Union and no summit. And had we not had that kind of security and that kind of secrecy that allowed for the kind of exchange that is essential, you men would still be in Hanoi, rather than Washington today. And let me say I think it is time in this country to quit making national heroes out of those who steal secrets and publish them in the newspaper.

THE VIETNAMESE VIEW

Amidst all the controversies, one thing is certain: the real losers of the Vietnam War were the South Vietnamese people. Five American presidents, Democrats and Republicans—Truman, Eisenhower, Kennedy, Johnson, and Nixon—strove to prevent that outcome, committing America's diplomatic, economic, and military support to that end. It took only one irresponsible Democrat Congress to throw it all away. To say that is not to make a partisan political statement, but to state a plain fact: the Democrat Congress of 1975, inebriated from having forced the resignation of Richard Nixon, kicked over the traces in Vietnam, divorcing America from its treaty commitments, and in an act as callow and selfish as any in political history decided that the best way to deal with South Vietnam was to jettison it—and leave it to be consumed by its Communist neighbor. John F. Kennedy's pledge to bear any burden and pay any price for the defense of liberty was squelched by the Democrats of '73 and '75, the first political manifestation, perhaps, of the liberal "me" generation.

Because Democrats have tried, outrageously, to present our scuttling of South Vietnam as moral and political wisdom, and as Hollywood and the liberal media have done the same, the voices of the South Vietnamese themselves have been largely ignored—despite the fact that Vietnamese-Americans, most of them refugees from the war, are today an important part of the American mosaic.

In the course of writing this book, I had the chance to meet an eloquent South Vietnamese refugee to this country, Major Hoi Ba Tran. Major Tran served twenty-two years in the Air Force of South Vietnam. He came to this country in 1975, the year his country was lost to the Communists. I offer this interview with him as a way to incorporate a voice that's not often heard in histories of the Vietnam War.

Jennings: Major Tran, what do you think are some of the bigger misconceptions of the early part of the Vietnam War?

Major Tran: Well, first of all, not many people spell the name of my country correctly; it is two words "Viet Nam." But more seriously, I think it is still not understood that Ho Chi Minh was not the popular nationalist some like to claim him to be, but was always a Communist and a blood-stained dictator like a Mao or a Stalin.

Jennings: What's your own take on the early years of the war?

Major Tran: To understand the conflict, you must at least go to the anti-colonial sentiment of Vietnam in the 1920s and 1930s. It was fervent, but the French were very effective at capturing, imprisoning, or executing Vietnamese patriots, and at putting down armed revolts. But with the support of the Chinese Nationalists, the Chinese Kuomintang Party—the party of Chiang Kai-shek—all Vietnamese Nationalist parties united under the name Viet Nam Cach Menh Dong Minh Hoi, which roughly translates as the Vietnamese Revolutionary Allied League. The Communist Party in Vietnam was already headed by Ho Chi Minh, and though the Nationalist Vietnamese had been brought together, in part, by Chiang Kai-shek, the Communist Mao Tse-Tung's enemy, Ho was also a member of the League.

Jennings: When was this?

Major Tran: Around 1930.

Jennings: What happened to Viet Nam in World War II?

Major Tran: Well, that was really the beginning of the end for the French. After France fell to the Nazis in 1940, we had a Vichy government in Vietnam. But the Japanese occupied the country anyway, and in March 1945, the Japanese launched a flash coup d'état and toppled the French government. The Japanese declared that Vietnam was an independent member of Japan's Greater East Asia Co-Prosperity Sphere, and they made a big deal about our being fellow Asians. But our superficial independence lasted only five months. A few days after Japan's surrender to the United States and the Allies, the Japanese military officials in Hanoi turned over the government to the Vietnamese local authority. But Ho Chi Minh had militia forces and armed propaganda units ready to topple local governments and seize power, which they did in Hanoi, and Ho formally declared the country to be the Democratic Republic of Vietnam. He proclaimed himself president and minister of Foreign Affairs. Vo Nguyen Giap, who would become his most famous general, was Minister of Interior.

Jennings: Did Ho have popular support?

Major Tran: No, but he tried to cultivate it—and to deceive Vietnamese nationalists and patriots—by concealing his Communist roots and inviting Emperor Bao Dai to be high counselor of his new government.

Jennings: It's often said that America's biggest mistake in Vietnam was not recognizing that Ho was a nationalist and pro-American, and we should have backed his government. I take it you don't agree.

Major Tran: No, and I can tell you a personal story about this. I was a ten-year-old boy when I saw Ho recite the Vietnamese Declaration of Independence in Ba Dinh Square in Hanoi. That was on September 2, 1945. Ho plagiarized his declaration from the American Declaration of Independence, which is why some Americans think Ho was pro-American. We were all cheering because we were overjoyed with this unexpected and sudden independence. I was part of what was called a Vanguard Youth Group. I held a small red flag with a yellow star in the middle—not knowing at the time it was a Communist flag. So even when Ho was plagiarizing the American Declaration of Independence, he was doing so as a Communist. I remember at the instruction of our leader, we waved the flag and sang a song we had been taught: "Who Loves Uncle Ho Chi Minh More than Us Young Children"—typical of the sort of ego-centric cult of personality that Communist leaders like Mao and Stalin pursued. Ho was a wily, evil person, and a devoted member of the International Communist Party.

Jennings: But was the Ho of the early years any more moderate than the Ho of the later years? Could he have been swayed?

Major Tran: No, his goal was always to put a Communist dictatorship over all of Vietnam. If Ho was a moderate, he would not have obeyed his Communist masters to run a so-called Land Reform Campaign that ordered the execution of about 50,000 landlords and the imprisonment of perhaps another 100,000. That was in the early 1950s. North Vietnam under Ho was a Communist police state.

Jennings: But Ho was willing to cut deals with the French right after World War II, right?

Major Tran: This only makes him more contemptible—he was a traitor; and you have to recognize his motivation. In 1946, Ho allowed French troops into Vietnam north of the 16th parallel in return for France recognizing his government. But he also had another motivation. The French troops were supposed to disarm the remaining Japanese. Before the French arrived, that job was being done by Chiang Kai-shek's forces. Ho wanted to get the anti-Communist Nationalist Chinese out of Vietnam. The Nationalist Chinese were sympathetic to the Nationalist Vietnamese, but Ho was not a nationalist but a Communist.

Jennings: And not a very bright one either—because the French decided to stay.

Major Tran: Of course they did. They believed we were still part of their empire. They declared that South Vietnam was to be under French control as the Republic of Cochinchina. Fighting broke out between the French and the Communist Viet Minh. A French warship even bombarded

Haiphong, a coastal city in North Vietnam, causing heavy casualties among the Viet Minh. All this was in 1946.

Jennings: If it was a choice between the French and the Communists, did the Vietnamese people prefer the French?

Major Tran: I am a Vietnamese nationalist, and we believed that was a false choice. We believed the French were brutal. But the Communists, of course, were much worse—murderous and totalitarian. It was very unfortunate that the French were defeated at Dien Bien Phu garrison. At least, however, the Geneva Agreement in 1954 divided Vietnam into two separate countries, so that the South, the Republic of Vietnam, would be free.

Jennings: But there was no chance Ho would accept that division.

Major Tran: No, but if he had been a true patriot he would have accepted it.

Jennings: Why?

Major Tran: A patriot would have dedicated himself to rebuilding his own country, the North Vietnam he inherited from the Japanese bloodlessly. Instead, he brought war and suffering to the people of Vietnam. If it were not for Ho and the Viet Minh, South Vietnam would have been peaceful and prosperous, but Ho refused to let the people in the South live peacefully and pursue their way of life.

Jennings: So the Vietnam War was a straightforward war of aggression by the North.

Major Tran: Yes, but it was also indisputably a proxy war between the superpowers. Ho Chi Minh could not have waged the war as he did without the support of the two Communist giants who were his patrons, the People's Republic of China and the Soviet Union. And of course the United States backed South Vietnam to contain Communist aggression.

Jennings: Could South Vietnam have won without America's help?

Major Tran: Not with all the support North Vietnam received from Communist China and the Soviet Union. And North Vietnam had certain advantages. It fought the war with no distractions. The Communist state could direct all its resources to fighting. It could thoroughly militarize its people. But we in the South were inevitably distracted by the results of our own freedom and of being an ally of America and the West, where it was taken for granted that you can protest, have open political opposition, and have a press that is hostile to the government. These are all valuable liberties, but it made governing and defending South Vietnam much more difficult because we had to defend ourselves not only against the Communists, but to our allies and our domestic and international critics. I think the West did not understand the difficulties South Vietnam faced transitioning from a traditional, feudal society into a Western democracy. The South was not given sufficient credit for trying—despite the difficulties, and even if imperfectly and only in stages—to become democratic.

In the North, the Communist Party, of course, controlled everything. Communist China and the Soviet Union were as dictatorial as North Vietnam and were completely supportive of the North Vietnamese jailing or liquidating any opposition. Life in North Vietnam was one of perpetual indoctrination, and the Communist troops were indoctrinated with hatred of America, and they presented the war as "Fighting the Americans to Save Our Country." In their people's armed forces, the political advisor had more authority than the unit commander did. And they knew they could exploit South Vietnam's freedom. Because the South had political dissidents, and students who were not indoctrinated and could express themselves, and Buddhists who had complaints against the government, the Communist underground cadres could infiltrate these groups and use them to trigger chaos and confusion. The same thing happened in America. In the end, the Communists kept their proxy in the proxy war, and the United States didn't.

Jennings: And why do you think that was?

Major Tran: Politics and the double-edged sword of freedom. Domestic unrest drove President Johnson from office, and President Nixon was compelled to negotiate with the Communists from a position of weakness, because Hanoi knew that the United States wanted to leave Vietnam. Hanoi only agreed to serious negotiations after its repeated efforts at military victory—like the TeT Offensive—ended in disaster, and after President Nixon and Dr. Henry Kissinger cleverly opened a diplomatic connection to China. Opening that connection was clever, but it also exposed—in fact Kissinger told the Chinese as much—that the United States did not seek to destroy or defeat the North Vietnamese Communists, but rather to end the war with some sort of political settlement that would preserve America's international reputation and appease domestic turmoil in America. Kissinger openly told the Chinese that the United States was more concerned about its relationship with China than with Saigon or Hanoi, or with Cambodia. He even envisioned that the United States could be on friendly relations with China and North Vietnam. He told his Chinese hosts that America could live with a Communist government in Indochina.

Jennings: But Hanoi didn't change its tune after Nixon's opening to China.

Major Tran: No, not right away. Nixon achieved that by force, with the Christmas bombing of 1972. The irony is that the Christmas bombing proved that the Communists could have been completely defeated, and yet the United States chose not to do so. For me, this is the most horrible thing to contemplate. The Christmas bombing brought Hanoi to its knees—many observers at the time recognized that—I was in Hanoi visiting my mother in 1998 after forty-four years and met many Hanoi residents who asserted the same—and yet, rather than press the campaign to its conclusion, the United States willingly declined a military victory, and was content to have further negotiations with Hanoi—and in those negotiations the United States did not even press to get terms that were more fair and reasonable for both sides, but merely settled for a peace agreement with dangerous provisions that left South Vietnam vulnerable for being defeated! What we were left with was President Nixon's promise of severe retaliation against Hanoi if it violated the Paris Agreement, which South Vietnam signed reluctantly on January 27, 1973. But Nixon's promises were almost immediately compromised. A few months following the signing of the Paris Agreement, the U.S. Congress passed an Amendment and a War Powers Act forbidding all U.S. military involvement in Southeast Asia. In 1974, President Nixon resigned because of the Watergate scandal, and then the U.S. Congress slashed military aid to South Vietnam. It was so drastic that we felt we had been abandoned. During this time, Communist China and the Soviet Union quadrupled their logistical support to Hanoi, paving the way for North Vietnam's invasion of South Vietnam in 1975.

Jennings: Well, Major, you now live in the United States. What would you like to tell young Vietnamese-Americans about the war?

Major Tran: I am glad you asked that, because I think it is very important that young Vietnamese-Americans know that we did our best, under terrible circumstances, to fight for democracy against Communism; they should be proud of their fathers and grandfathers. I would also like to tell my Vietnamese brothers-in-arms that of course our country and our army were imperfect. We had our share of inept political leaders as well as incompetent field commanders; and of course our leaders' hands were sometimes tied behind their backs by our own ally. Yet we fought courageously against overwhelming odds and hundreds of thousands of our friends lost their lives in a just cause. We did not win because the outcome was determined by superpower politics. Obviously it was way beyond the soldier's responsibility. If we, the Republic of Vietnam, had it our way, if we rather than Kissinger had been negotiating our future, unquestionably, the outcome of the war would have been different.

Jennings: And do you have a message for Americans who fought in the war?

Major Tran: Of course. To my American brothers-in-arms I would say you fought courageously and well. It was your politicians who settled the war politically, who ordered you to withdraw from Vietnam, and, ironically, gave away the victory you had won. The last U.S. military unit left Vietnam in March 1973. The final collapse of South Vietnam occurred on April 30, 1975. There is absolutely no doubt in my mind that the United States did not lose the war in Vietnam militarily; only ignorant or misled individuals could say that. You fulfilled the call of duty admirably. We salute you. We thank you for serving and for helping us in Vietnam.

Victorious Boat People

I should perhaps add one final note here, that some of the ironic winners of the Vietnam War are the brave Boat People who escaped Communist Vietnam to make a new life here in the United States. Before 1975, only a few thousand Vietnamese lived in America. According to the most recent State Department survey, they are now the fourth largest minority population in America, about 1.5 million people.

When Saigon fell in 1975, those Vietnamese who were determined to seek liberty and freedom from political oppression fled their native land. "[The] United States extended its generous hand, accepting thousands of Vietnamese refugees as citizens of this great nation."[1] These words were written by one of those refugees.

From 1978 to 1982, a repressive movement against Vietnamese of Chinese descent caused another wave of "boat people." Their slogan was "Freedom or Die." According to the United States High Commission for Refugees, an estimated 700,000 of these boat people died at sea.[2]

Those South Vietnamese who could not escape and who were connected to the United States or the military were often subjected to brutal treatment, including almost certain imprisonment for all former military personnel—the sentences ranging from months to fifteen years, depending on rank. After hard labor during the day, they attended evening classes to be indoctrinated with Marxist and Leninist theories in order to remove any "imperialistic residue." If they were not cooperative, they could be tortured.

ARVN Major Nguyen had worked for the CIA and could not leave Vietnam because of an ailing mother. He was in solitary confinement for more than nine years, often incarcerated in a small hole dug in the ground. He was unrepentant and refused to denounce the South Vietnamese or American governments. Finally released in the tenth year, he walked from the Hanoi area to his home in Saigon. A week later he was arrested again and shipped back to his hole outside Hanoi for two more years. The Communists believed that seeing his family might break him. It did not, and he resides in Texas now. He is ardently pro-American, saying that "American soldiers fought with us and died with us. I am thankful for them."[3]

The Vietnamese have entered into and prospered in every sector of American society. In 2005, the combined income of 2 million Vietnamese Americans equaled the entire national income of Vietnam, a country of 80 million people.

I had the privilege of meeting Major Nguyen when he finally stepped off the airplane in Dallas, eleven years after he was captured by the North Vietnamese. He told me that he was so proud of never giving in to the Communists and never denouncing America. He also told me that he would never forget America's sacrifice for him and his country, and how happy he was that he had been accepted here as an immigrant.

A friend of his, Major Ninh, had escaped Saigon in 1975 with his extended family on a boat. His wife was raped and beaten when they landed ashore in Indonesia, and one of his daughters was kidnapped at sea and never seen again. This great gentleman was proud that he now had two companies, one a cleaning company and one a pillow factory;

Give Me Your ARVN Yearning to Breathe Free

South Vietnamese veterans endured the loss of their country. Many endured the additional perils of becoming "boat people." But for those who made it here—however tinged with wrenching sadness, separated from a land, a people, and family that they loved—there was this reward: they became citizens of the freest country in the world, and they and their children and grandchildren have prospered wonderfully.

his oldest daughter has a computer repair shop, and his son was a West Point graduate finishing a tour as a Ranger. For Major Ninh, Major Tran, and so many others, the pain of defeat was as bitter, as horrible, as could be. But they could not have predicted—and they could not be more thankful for—the second chance they have been given. They know better than anyone what America was fighting for in Vietnam; they have found it here.

BIBLIOGRAPHY

"Vietnam War Statistics." July 7, 2009. *http://vietnamresearch.com/history/ stats.html.*

Allen, George W. *None So Blind: A Personal Account of the Intelligence Failure in Vietnam.* Chicago, IL: Ivan R. Dee, 2001.

Anderson, David L. and John Ernst. *The War That Never Ends.* Lexington, KY: The University Press of Kentucky, 2007.

Andrade, Dale. *America's Last Vietnam Battle: Halting Hanoi's 1972 Easter Offensive.* Lawrence, KS: University Press of Kansas, 2001.

Appy, Christian G. *Patriots: The Vietnam War Remembered From All Sides.* New York, NY: Viking Penguin, 2003.

"Assorted Memorandums." July 7, 2009. *http://www.ford.utexas.edu/library/ exhibits/vietnam/750512b.jpg.*

Atwood, Paul, B.A., M.A., Ph.D. "Secret Bombing of Cambodia." *Microsoft Encarta Online Encyclopedia.* July 23, 2009. *http://encarta.msn.com.*

Blakey, Scott. *Prisoner At War: The Survival of Commander Richard A. Stratton.* Garden City, NY: Anchor Press/Doubleday, 1978.

Bonior, David E., Steven M. Champlin, and Timothy S. Kolly. *The Vietnam Veteran: A History of Neglect.* New York, NY: Praeger Publishers, 1984.

Bordenkircher, D. E. and S. A. Bordenkircher. *Tiger Cage: An Untold Story.* Cameron, WV: Abby Publishing, 1998.

Braestrup, Peter. *Big Story.* New Haven, CT: Yale University Press, 1978.

Burkett, B. G. and Glenna Whitley. *Stolen Valor*. Dallas, TX: Verity Press, Inc., 1998.

Buzzango, Robert. *Masters of War*. New York, NY: Cambridge University Press, 1996.

Castle, Timothy N. *One Day Too Long*. New York, NY: Columbia University Press, 1999.

Castle, Timothy N. *One Day Too Long: Top Secret Site 85 and the Bombing of North Vietnam*. New York, NY: Columbia University Press, 1999.

Chomsky, Noam. "The Legacy of the Vietnam War." August 9, 2009. *http://www.chomsky.info/interviews/198210—.htm*.

Colby, William. *Lost Victory*. Chicago, IL: Contemporary Books, 1989.

Courtois, Stephane, Nicolas Werth, Jean-Louis Panne, Andrezej Paczkowski, Karel Bartosek, and Jean-Louis Margolin. *The Black Book of Communism*. Cambridge, MA: Harvard University Press, 1999.

Currey, Cecil B. *Victory at Any Cost*. Washington, D.C.: Potomac Books, Inc., 1997.

Dallek, Robert. *Nixon and Kissinger*. New York, NY: HarperCollins Publishers, 2007.

Davidson, Phillip B. *Vietnam at War: The History 1946-1975*. New York, NY: Oxford University Press, 1991.

Diem, Bui and David Chanoff. *In The Jaws of History*. Bloomington, IN: Indiana University Press, 1987.

Downs, Frederick. *No Longer Enemies, Not Yet Friends*. New York, NY: W.W. Norton & Company, 1991.

Duiker, William J. *Ho Chi Minh: A Life*. New York, NY: Hyperion, 2000.

Dunnigan, James F. and Albert A. Nofi. *Dirty Little Secrets of the Vietnam War*. New York, NY: Thomas Dunne Books, 1999.

Efaw, Fritz. "Chickenhawks, Draft Dodgers and War Resisters." August 21, 2009. *http://www.vvaw.org/veteran/article/?id=351*.

Ellsberg, Daniel. *Secrets: A Memoir of Vietnam and the Pentagon Papers*. New York, NY: Penguin Books, 2002.

Bibliography

Ely, John Hart. *War and Responsibility*. Princeton, NJ: Princeton University Press, 1993.

Fall, Bernard B. *Street Without Joy*. London, England: Pall Mall Press, 1964.

Franklin, H. Bruce. *Vietnam & Other American Fantasies*. Amherst, MA: University of Massachusetts Press, 2000.

Frankum Jr., Ronald B. *Like Rolling Thunder: The Air War in Vietnam 1964-1975*. Lanham, MD: Rowman and Littlefield Publishers, Inc., 2005.

Friedman, Herbert. "Weapons of Mass Persuasion." In *Vietnam*. October 2009: 38–42.

Gettleman, Marvin E., Jane Franklin, Marilyn B. Young, and H. Bruce Franklin. *Vietnam and America: A Documented History*. New York, NY: Grove Press, 1995.

Giap, General Vo Nguyen. *Big Victory, Great Task*. New York, NY: Frederick A. Praeger, 1968.

Giap, General Vo Nguyen. *How We Won the War*. Philadelphia, PA: Recon Publications, 1976.

Gilbert, Marc Jason. *Why the North Won the Vietnam War*. New York, NY: Palgrave, 2002.

Hearden, Patrick J. *The Tragedy of Vietnam*. New York, NY: Pearson Longman, 2005.

Hendrickson, Paul. *The Living and the Dead*. New York, NY: Vintage Books, 1996.

Herring, George C. *The Pentagon Papers: Abridged Edition*. United States of America: McGraw-Hill, Inc., 1993.

Hershberger, Mary. *Jane Fonda's War*. New York, NY: The New Press, 2005.

Hitchens, Christopher. *The Trial of Henry Kissinger*. New York, NY: Verso, 2002.

Holzer, Henry Mark, and Erika Holzer. *Aid and Comfort: Jane Fonda in North Vietnam*. Jefferson, NC: McFarland & Company, Inc., 2002.

Karnow, Stanley. *Vietnam: A History*. New York, NY: The Viking Press, 1983.

Kimball, Jeffrey. *The Vietnam War Files: Uncovering the Secret History of Nixon-Era Strategy*. Lawrence, KS: University Press of Kansas, 2004.

Kissinger, Henry. *Ending the Vietnam War*. New York, NY: Simon & Schuster, 2003.

Kissinger, Henry. *White House Years*. Boston, MA: Little, Brown and Company, 1979.

Leaf, Jonathan. *The Politically Incorrect Guide™ to The Sixties*. Washington, D.C.: Regnery Publishing, Inc., 2009.

Lehrack, Otto J. *The First Battle: Operation Starlite and the Beginning of the Blood Debt in Vietnam*. Haverton, PA: Casemate, 2004.

Lewy, Guenter. *America in Vietnam*. New York, NY: Oxford University Press, 1980.

Lind, Michael. *Vietnam: The Necessary War*. New York, NY: Touchstone, 1999.

Macdonald, Peter. *Giap*. New York, NY: W.W. Norton & Company, 1993.

Maclear, Michael. *The Ten Thousand Day War: Vietnam 1945-1975*. New York, NY: St. Martin's Press, 1981.

McMahon, Robert J. *Major Problems in the History of the Vietnam War*. Boston, MA: Houghton Mifflin Company, 2003.

McMaster, H.R. *Dereliction of Duty*. New York, NY: HarperPerennial, 1998.

McNamara, Robert S. *In Retrospect: The Tragedy and Lessons of Vietnam*. New York, NY: Times Books, 1995.

McNamara, Robert S., James G. Blight, and Robert K. Brigham. *Argument Without End*. New York, NY: PublicAffairs, 1999.

Meilinger, Phillip S. "Turbulence Over Vietnam." *Vietnam* June 2009: 52-57.

Moyar, Mark. *Triumph Forsaken: The Vietnam War, 1954-1965*. New York, NY: Cambridge University Press, 2006.

Mueller, John E. *War, Presidents and Public Opinion*. New York, NY: John Wiley & Sons, Inc., 1973.

Nalty, Bernard C. *The Vietnam War*. New York, NY: Barnes & Noble Books, 1998.

Nelson, Deborah. *The War Behind Me*. Philadelphia, PA: Basic Books, 2008.

Nichols, Cdr. John B. USN (Ret.) and Barrett Tillman. *On Yankee Station*. Annapolis, MD: Naval Institute Press, 1987.

Nixon, Richard. *No More Vietnams*. New York, NY: Arbor House, 1985.

"North Vietnam's Master Plan." August 9, 2009. *http://www.historynet.com/north-vietnams-master-plan.htm.*

Olson, James S. and Randy Roberts. *My Lai.* Boston, MA: Bedford Books, 1998.

Olson, James S. and Randy Roberts. *Where the Domino Fell: America and Vietnam, 1945-1990.* New York, NY: St. Martin's Press, 1991.

Palmer, Dave R. *Summons of the Trumpet.* Novato, CA: Presidio Press, 1978.

Phillips, Rufus. *Why Vietnam Matters.* Annapolis, MD: Naval Institute Press, 2008.

Podhoretz, Norman. *Why We Were in Vietnam.* New York, NY: Simon and Schuster, 1982.

Prados, John. *Safe for Democracy.* Chicago, IL: Ivan R. Dee, 2006.

Prados, John. *William Colby and the CIA: The Secret Wars of a Controversial Spymaster.* Lawrence, KS: University Press of Kansas, 2009.

Pulvers, Roger. "Ghosts of Christmas Past: The Christmas Bombing of Vietnam." *Zmag* January 3, 2007. *ZNet.* April 19, 2009. *http://www.zmag.org/znet/viewArticle/2387.*

Randolph, Stephen P. *Powerful and Brutal Weapons: Nixon, Kissinger, and the Easter Offensive.* Cambridge, MA: Harvard University Press, 2007.

Robbins, Christopher. *The Ravens: The Men Who Flew in America's Secret War in Laos.* New York, NY: Crown Publishers, Inc., 1987.

Rochester, Stuart I. and Frederick Kiley. *Honor Bound: American Prisoners of War in Southeast Asia 1961-1973.* Annapolis, MD: Naval Institute Press, 1999.

Rodman, Peter W. "Sideswipe: Kissinger, Shawcross and the Responsibility for Cambodia." In *The American Spectator* March 1981: 7–15.

Rodman, Peter W. *Presidential Command.* New York, NY: Alfred A. Knopf, 2009.

Sesser, Stan. *The Lands of Charm and Cruelty.* New York, NY: Alfred A. Knopf, 1993.

Shawcross, William. *Sideshow: Kissinger, Nixon and the Destruction of Cambodia.* New York, NY: Pocket Books, 1979.

Sheehan, Neil, Hendrick Smith, E. W. Kenworthy, and Fox Butterfield. *The Pentagon Papers.* New York, NY: Bantam Books, Inc., 1971.

Sorley, Lewis. *A Better War*. Orlando, FL: Harcourt, Inc., 1999.

Spector, Ronald H. *After Tet*. New York, NY: Vintage Books, 1994.

Thai, Vu Van. "A Regional Solution for Viet Nam." 3 August 2009 *http://www.foreignaffairs.com/articles/23953/vu-van-thai/a-regional-solution-for-viet-nam*.

"The Tet Offensive 1968." *The Vietnam Experience Nineteen Sixty-Eight*. 25 July 2009 *http://diggerhistory.info/pages-conflicts-periods/vietnam/tet.htm*.

Timberg, Robert. *The Nightingale's Song*. New York, NY: Touchstone, 1995.

Van Canh, Nguyen with Earle Cooper. *Vietnam Under Communism, 1975-1982*. Stanford, CA: Hoover Institution Press, 1983.

Webb, James. "Heroes of the Vietnam Generation."

West, Captain Francis J., USMCR. *Small Unit Action in Vietnam: Summer 1966*. New York, NY: Arno Press, Inc., 1967.

Westmoreland, General William C. *A Soldier Reports*. Garden City, NY: Doubleday & Company, Inc., 1976.

Willbanks, James H. *Abandoning Vietnam: How America Left and South Vietnam Lost Its War*. Lawrence, KS: University Press of Kansas, 2008.

Woods, Jr., Ph.D., Thomas E. *The Politically Incorrect Guide™ to American History*. Washington, DC: Regnery Publishing, 2004.

NOTES

Introduction

The Defeat That Wasn't

1. *Vietnam War: History*, BBC News; available online at: http://news.bbc.co.uk/2/shared/spl/hi/asia_pac/05/vietnam_war/html/introduction.stm (accessed December 31, 2009).

2. Duncan Currie, "Not Your Father's Vietnam," T*he American*, January 11, 2007.

Chapter 1

Why We Were in Vietnam

1. 20 Years After Victory, April 1995, Folder 14, Box 24, Douglas Pike Collection: Unit 06 - Democratic Republic of Vietnam, The Vietnam Archive, Texas Tech University.

2. Robert A. Nisbet, *Roosevelt and Stalin: The Failed Courtship* (Washington, D.C.: Regnery Publishing, 1989).

3. A. J. Langguth, *Our Vietnam: The War 1954-1975* (New York: Simon and Schuster, 2000).

4. Mark E. Cunningham and Lawrence J. Zwier, *The Aftermath of French Defeat in Vietnam (Aftermath of History)* (Breckenridge, CO: Twentyfirst Century Books, 2009), 18.

5. Robert McMahon, *Major Problems in the History of the Vietnam War* (Orlando, FL: Houghton Mifflin), 83.

6. Mark Moyar, Triumph Forsaken (New York: Cambridge University Press, 2006), 29.

7. Ibid., 35.

8. Phillip Davidson, *Vietnam at War* (New York: Oxford University Press, 1988), 288.

9. Mark Moyar, *Triumph Forsaken*, 46.

10. William E. Colby and James McCargar, *Lost Victory: A Firsthand Account of America's Sixteen-Year Involvement in Vietnam* (Chicago, IL: Contemporary Books, 1989).

11. Mark Moyar, *Triumph Forsaken*, 45.

12. Ibid., 59.

13. William E. Colby and James McCargar, *Lost Victory*.

14. Ibid.

15. Ibid.

16. Mark Moyar, *Triumph Forsaken*, 81.

17. Ibid., 81.

18. Phillip B. Davidson *Vietnam at War*, 289.

19. Ibid.

Chapter 2

Camelot It Was Not

1. Mark Moyar, *Triumph Forsaken*, 133.

2. Michael McClintock, *Instruments of Statecraft; U.S. Guerrilla Warfare, Counterinsurgency, and Counter Terrorism, 1940-1990.*

3. Ibid.

4. William J. Duiker, *Ho Chi Minh: A Life* (New York: Hyperion, 2000).

5. Remarks of Senator John F. Kennedy at the Conference on Vietnam Luncheon in the Hotel Willard, Washington, D.C., June 1, 1956.

6. Ibid.

7. Mark Moyar, *Triumph Forsaken*.

8. Ibid.

9. Ibid.

10. Ibid., 185.

11. Ibid.

12. Lewis Sorley, *A Better War: The Unexamined Victories and Final Tragedy of America's Last Years in Vietnam* (Orlando, FL: Harcourt Inc., 1999), 348.

13. Mark Moyar, *Triumph Forsaken*.

14. Ibid.

15. Ibid.

16. William E. Colby and James McCargar, *Lost Victory*.

17. Mark Moyar, *Triumph Forsaken*, 241.

18. Robert Dallek, *An Unfinished Life: John F. Kennedy 1917–1963* (Boston, MA: Little, Brown and Company, May 2003).

19. Mark Moyar, *Triumph Forsaken*.

20. Ibid., 250.

21. Ibid., 286.

22. *Department of State Central Files, POL 26 S. Vietnam Embassy in Vietnam to Dept of State, Nov 1, 1963*.

23. Robert Osgood, *Limited War Revisited* (Westview Press, 1979).

Chapter 3

LBJ's War

1. Robert F. Turner, "How the Vietnam War started," *Washington Times*, August 2, 2009.

2. Phillip Davidson, *Vietnam at War*, 320.

3. Southeast Asia Collective Defense Treaty.

4. U.S. Military various

5. Peter Brush, "The Story Behind the McNamara Line" *Vietnam*, February 1996.

6. Phillip Davidson, *Vietnam at War*.

7. Bui Diem and David Chanoff, *In the Jaws of History* (Bloomington, IN: Indiana University Press, 1987), 131.

8. Otto J. Lehrack, *The First Battle* (Havertown, PA: Casemate, 2004).

9. Ibid.

10. Ibid.

11. Mona Charen, *Useful Idiots* (Washington, D.C.: Regnery Publishing, 2003), 33.

12. Phillip Davidson, *Vietnam at War*, 362.

13. Mark Moyar, *Triumph Forsaken The Vietnam War, 1954-1965* (New York: Cambridge University Press, 2006), 301.

14. Phillip Davidson, *Vietnam at War*, 314.

15. Pentagon Papers.

16. Lyndon B. Johnson papers.

17. Ibid.

18. Phillip Davidson, *Vietnam at* War, 322.

19. Ibid., 336.

20. Jacob Van Staaveren, *Interdiction in Southern Laos, 1961-1968* (Washington, D.C.: Center of Air Force History, 1993), 287.

21. Jonah Goldberg, "There Are Tears in my Eyes—Eddie Adams & the Most Famous Photo of the Vietnam War," *National Review Online*, August 26, 1999.

22. Confederate Lt. General in the Civil War.

23. Peter Braestrup, *Big Story* (New Haven, CT: Yale University Press, 1978).

24. Ibid.

25. Ibid.

26. Hanoi Government Press Release, Agence France Presse, April 3, 1995.

27. Norman Podhoretz, *Why We Were in Vietnam* (New York: Simon and Schuster, 1982), 110.

28. Lt. General Charles G. Cooper, *Cheers and Tears: A Marine's Story of Combat in Peace and War* (Wesley Press: 2002).

Chapter 4

Unheralded Victory

1. David R. Palmer, *Summons of the Trumpet: U.S.-Vietnam in Perspective* (Novato, CA: Presidio Press, 1978), 180.

2. Lewis Sorley, *A Better War*, 14.

3. Ibid., 24.

4. John F. Kennedy Inaugural Speech

5. William E. Colby, *Lost Victory* (Chicago, IL: Contemporary Books, 1989).

6. Ibid.

7. Lewis Sorley, *A Better War*.

8. Leslie Gelb, Director of the Pentagon Papers project.

9. Ibid.

10. David R. Palmer, *Summons of the Trumpet*, 223.

11. William E. Colby and James McCargar, *Lost Victory*.

12. Ibid., 245.

13. Lewis Sorley, *A Better War*, 147.

14. Lewis Sorley, *A Better War*, 384.

15. Ibid., 146.

16. Henry Kissinger, *Ending the Vietnam War: A History of American Involvement in and Extraction From the Vietnam War* (New York: Simon and Schuster, 2003).

17. Lewis Sorley, *A Better War*.

18. Henry Kissinger, *White House Years* (Boston, MA: Little, Brown and Company, 1979), 237.

19. Ibid.

20. Patrick J. Hearden, *The Tragedy of Vietnam* (New York, NY: Pearson Longman, 2005).

21. Ibid.

22. Lewis Sorley, *A Better War*.

23. Henry Kissinger, *White House Years*.

24. Kenton Clymer, *The U.S. and Cambodia Vol. II 1969-2000* (Routledge, 2004).

25. Nguyen Van Canh, *Vietnam Under Communism 1975-1982*.

26. A Personal Interview with the Author.

27. Phillip Davidson, *Vietnam at War*.

29. Henry Kissinger, *White House Years*, 498.

28. Phillip Davidson, *Vietnam at War*.

30. Richard M. Nixon, Speech, January 4, 1971.

31. Richard M. Nixon, conversation with Henry Kissinger.

32. Robert S. McNamara, *In Retrospect: The Tragedy and Lessons of Vietnam* (New York: Times Books, 1995).

33. Robert Dallek, *Nixon and Kissinger* (New York, NY: HarperCollins Publishers, 2007), 446.

34. Henry Kissinger, *White House Years*, 728.

35. Martin Herz, "The Prestige Press and the Christmas Bombing 1972," *New York Times*, May 1, 1975.

36. Robert Dallek, *Nixon and Kissinger*, 446.

37. Combat Area Casualty File, November 1993, Vietnam Veterans' Memorial. Center for Electronic Records, National Archives, Washington, DC.

38. *Ending the Vietnam War*, Kissinger, Simon and Schuster, 2003, p. 116.

39. Nguyen Van Canh, *Vietnam Under Communism* 1975-1982 (Stanford, CA: Hoover Institution Press, 1983).

40. Henry Kissinger, *White House Years*.

41. Bui Diem and David Chanoff, *In the Jaws of History*.

42. Cecil B. Currey, *Victory at Any Cost: The Genius of Viet Nam's General Giap* (New York, NY: Brassey's, 1996).

43. General Vo Nguyen Giap, *How We Won the War* (Philadelphia, PA: Recon Publications, 1976).

44. Henry Kissinger, *The White House Years, 228*.

Chapter 5

The Anti-War Movement

1. Ion Mihai Pacepa, "The highest ranking intelligence officer ever to defect from the Soviet Bloc," *National Review*, February 22. 2004.

2. Mark Moyar, *Triumph Forsaken*.

3. Mary Hershberger, *Jane Fonda's War* (New York: The New Press, 2005).

4. Ibid.

5. Guenther Lewy, *America in Vietnam* (New York: Oxford University Press, 1980).

6. B. G. Burkett and Glenna Whitley, *Stolen Valor* (Dallas, TX: Verity Press, 1998).

7. Ibid.

8. Ibid.

9. Marvin E. Gettleman, Jane Franklin, Marilyn B. Young, and H. Bruce Franklin, *Vietnam and America: A Documented History* (New York, NY: Grove Press, 1995).

10. John Stuart Mill, *On Liberty* (New York: Dover Publications, 2002).

11. Mary Hershberger, *Jane Fonda's War*.

12. John E. Mueller, *War, Presidents, and Public Opinion* (New York, NY: John Wiley and Sons, Inc., 1973), 72–98.

13. Vietnam Helicopter Flight Crew Network, "Statistics about the Vietnam War" available online at http://www.vhfcn.org/stat.html (accessed January 2010).

14. Henry Kissinger, *White House Years.*

15. Primarily from an interview by Paul Shannon, published in *The Indo-China Newsletter*, Issue 18, Nov–Dec, p. 1–5, October 1982.

16. Scott Swett and Roger Canfield, "Obama's Foul Weather Friends," *American Thinker*, September 16, 2008; available online at: http://www.americanthinker.com/2008/09/obamas_foul_weather_friends.html, (accessed January 2010).

17. Ibid.

Chapter 6
Coming Home

1. Stuart I. Rochester and Frederick Kiley, *Honor Bound: American Prisoners of War in Southeast Asia,* 1961–1963 (Annapolis, MD: Naval Institute Press, 1999).

2. Ibid.

3. Ibid.

4. Ibid.

5. Col. Robbie Risner, *The Passing of the Night: My Seven Years as a Prisoner of the North Vietnamese* (NY: Random House, 1974).

6. Earnest C. Brace, *A Code to Keep: The True Story of America's Longest Held Civilian Prisoner of War in Vietnam* (NY: St. Martin's Press, 1988).

7. Scott Blakey, *Prisoner at War: The Survival of Commander Richard A. Stratton* (Garden City, NY: Anchor Press/Doubleday, 1978).

8. Lawrence Bailey, *Solitary Survivor: The First American P.O.W. in Southeast Asia* (Potoma Books, Inc., 2003).

9. John E. Mueller, War, *Presidents and Public Opinion.*

10. James Webb, "Freedom Hero: Heroes of the Vietnam Generation," *The American Enterprise*, September 2000.

INDEX